JUST BRAVE IT

Just Brave it

A SOME-NONSENSE GUIDE FOR WOMEN WHO WANT TO LIVE A BRAVE AND FULFILLING LIFE

AMY DRUHOT

ISBN: 979-8-9902141-0-1 (paperback)
ISBN: 979-8-9902141-1-8 (hardcover)
ISBN: 979-8-9902141-2-5 (ebook)

Cover Design by Wizdiz (99Designs)

Interior Design by Six Penny Graphics

For key-note inquiries or book orders at special quantity discounts contact justbraveitbook@gmail.com or visit www.amydruhot.com.

This book is dedicated to:

Amelia Freaking O'Connor, you saw me first.
I still want to be you when I grow up.

The OG WLC, you are the bravest women I know.

The women I've served, the women I currently serve
and the women I have yet to serve. I love you. I see you.
I appreciate you. This book is for you. (PWB-RVA)

And Emily Feagles, who wrote me an email saying, "I
cannot wait for your book to come out. I am so intrigued
by your story," confirming that I would sell at least one
copy so I should hurry and get to finishing this thang up.

Contents

Preface

Brilliant is a word I often use to describe other people I look up to as being good at their craft. It's also a word I never use to describe myself. I'm not brilliant or genius. In fact, I'm quite ordinary. I shouldn't be as successful as I am, and Lord knows I shouldn't be writing a book that anyone should read for purpose of growth or inspiration. Truth is, if Brené Brown is Saks 5th Avenue, then I'm freaking Target, y'all.

I didn't go to college. High school graduate...eh, debatable? I've gotten life wrong a (whole) lot and I've had to completely embrace fear because I spent a lot of time being afraid that I wasn't worthy of the life I wanted to live.

So how did I end up here? VP title, board and president seats on industry councils, Virginia's Woman of the Year for my industry, invitations to speak and even get paid for it (what the even heck?!?...I'm still in shock myself), someone whom other women reach out to for counsel and advice?

I didn't map it out or plan it, but it did take discovering my "why" to live an uncompromising life centered in purpose. (I like to refer to this as my "impact why.") And if I can do it, then you can too.

I may not be brilliant, but I know who I am and I know the impact I want to make in the world. Those things are the secret ingredients to living a life of not just success, but fulfillment.

If you think you can't because you don't have the advantages of those accomplishing the things you dream about—think again. Undereducated (✓) Single Mother (✓) Divorcee (✓) Laid off (✓) Housecleaner (✓) Victim (Nope) Excuse Maker (Nope) Negative Thinker (Nope) Sit Arounder and wait for the world to come to me (Nope, Nope, Nope).

If you're ordinary like me, I hope this book helps you find your purpose and start braving the things you would do or try if you knew for a fact that you couldn't fail. And for those of you who are brilliant geniuses already succeeding at your craft, who knows? Maybe there's something here for you too.

What if we all were brave enough to start thinking in terms of what we would accomplish if we thought we couldn't fail? How much further would we all go? Regardless of our past, experience, or background.

Three simple words drive this idea in life for me. Three words I live by, rest on, and use to propel me toward the life I live and want.

Just Brave It.

BRAVE IT

til you

MAKE IT

Introduction

Ever see someone trip and fall? Only they don't just fall. Their fall is more of a series of missteps in sequence, fumbling one after the other as if it will never end until...BAM...they end up on their tush and announce to anyone who's listening, "I'm OK."

Well, welcome to my life. That's the best way to describe it, both literally and figuratively. I just fell into this, fumbling the whole way down. It all kinda happened by accident. I don't have impostor syndrome. I actually AM an impostor. I'm not supposed to be here. I mean, who decides to write a book when they can count the number of books they've actually read on one hand?? (I just raised my own hand.)

We can't be good at everything. I'm a better writer than a reader, and I'm OK with that. So what qualifies me? I'm also a better live-er than reader. No research, no self-help books—I've just lived. But in doing so, I've learned. And believe me, I'm not saying I'm an expert because I've done a lot right. Yeah, um, no. Unfortunately for me that wasn't the case. Just braving it was not some mantra I came up with in fourth grade while in Girl Scouts nor was it something I started telling myself when I entered adulthood and decided what I wanted to do with my life. Just brave it was just something that happened. Unintentionally, over, and over.

It wasn't until a year or so ago that the phrase even came to fruition during what would be one of the most embarrassing moments of my life. (I'll save that story for later in the book, but trust me, if you stick around long enough to get to it you'll be glad you did). But in speaking, or in the true sense of how it went down, "announcing" that I was "just gonna brave it," I realized that "braving it" was what I had been doing all along.

We've all heard the phrase "Fake it till you make it." I used to think that was me...blasphemy! I "Brave it till I make it." Because isn't that what we're doing? It takes being brave to put ourselves in situations where we have no clue what we're doing and yet need to appear that we do. We all do it. From the brilliant to the ordinary.

I overcame and accomplished a lot before I ever muttered that mantra. But when I became intentional about just braving it, I started living bigger and believing in myself differently. And I continue to do that every day. Tell the girl who 13 years ago was cleaning houses for a living that she would hold a vice president title, start councils to support women in a male-dominated industry, be named Woman of the Year and be asked to speak in front of groups of women to share her story, and she would have never believed you. Tell that same girl today that she can write a book and influence others to believe they can do the same and she has no doubt. So here I am writing that book and here you are reading it.

I was afraid of sharing my story because I struggled with believing that I was inspirational. I'm good at messing up. I didn't feel worthy of inspiring others until recently when someone said something to me that completely changed my way of thinking. He said, "You don't get to choose if you're inspirational or not; others do."

It took such a weight off me. I didn't need to "try" to be inspirational. I just needed to be me. It's like me telling someone "I'm funny." That's great and all but if I can't make you laugh, then I'm simply not funny. If people say you're inspirational, all you have to do is show up and be you; that's who they're already expecting you to be. People want to be inspired.

My story is worthy of inspiring. And yours is too. I hope my story not only inspires you to think bigger, live bigger, and brave it, but it also helps you to embrace your own story. That you seek out the past moments of bravery and recognize them for that, being brave. And that you continue to seek out opportunities to just brave it.

You are worthy of the life you want, regardless of your experience, background, education, or any other hand you've been dealt. We get one life—why are we all not chasing after our wildest dreams like we're on fire?

So, I'll start by asking you—What would you do, for real, if you thought you absolutely, positively could not fail? Seriously. If you can answer that but you're doing nothing to work toward whatever it is, then this book is for you. If you can't answer the question and need some inspiration, then this book is also for you. Or if you're already living your dreams and braving it every day, then you're probably one of the people I refer to as brilliant and this book is also for you. You hold the power to help and inspire others. I hope that in sharing my story it inspires you to also do the same.

WHY POWER

>

will power

CHAPTER ONE:

Friedrich Nietzsche once said, "He who has a *why* to live for can bear almost any *how*." Someone else also once said, "Having a *why* is as cheesy as Cheetos covered in queso with shredded cheese on top." (Spoiler alert: It was me. I said it).

Find your *why*. Connect to your *why*. What is the one word to describe your *why? Why, why, why?* (Translation: barf, barf, barf.) Now, I can get on board with feeling radical about something, but the whole "Discover your why" felt as outdated as Myspace. Yes, the background music and selfie picture slide show felt good at the time but, most all would agree, it's cringe-worthy today.

"Why" was hard for me. Really? We're all supposed to narrow our complete existence to one singular word. It just didn't seem possible. How can one *person, place, thing, or word* sum up what gets my mojo going in the morning? It all just seemed like a bunch of bologna if you asked me. (Autocorrect wanted me to change it to "bolognas." I guess because I said "a bunch." Just wanted y'all to know I'm not holding back on you. You can have all the bologna you want, piles and piles, but for the sake of my point, I'm only giving you one, slice that is, of bologna in the bunch.)

2022 was a transformational year for me. I signed up for a women's leadership roundtable, which was the first all-female mastermind group in my industry. I started the first Professional Women in Building Council in Virginia. I was asked to be on an executive leadership team for a movement in our industry to advocate for females and underrepresented individuals in construction. I decided to get my certification in Diversity, Equity, and Inclusion from Cornell University. I started initiatives in my local market for other women to make an impact and was named as Woman of the Year for our state's association.

I was starting what felt like a calling, to help to create a space for women in construction, but doing it all without true purpose. I mean, I knew I was chipping away at the rock one hit at a time, but I wasn't sure what I was *actually* creating. It all sounded like a lot, but what was my real impact? Could I point to one singular woman in my industry and say I changed things for the better for her? I wasn't sure I could.

It wasn't until about a year ago, when I was in Florida at a sales training conference for my industry, that I was able to hear a dear friend, David Hagen, speak. In his presentation he began talking about his *why*. He spoke about his father, whom he'd recently lost. I, too, had recently lost my father. It hit like Mike Tyson on his best day. Ever been at church and the preacher is giving his sermon and it has you sweatin' like a ho in church because you're convinced he's had someone following you and the message was personalized just for you and your sins? Yeah, I was there, sweaty armpits and all. (Even my eyes were sweatin', if you know what I mean.)

And y'all... I. Was. Moved.

I might as well have been at the First Southern Baptist Church of *Why*. If there was an altar call for giving your life to your *why* at the end of his talk, I would have been the first one up front falling on my knees. For the first time in a long time, I understood the importance of our *why*. It was then in that moment that I understood that:

Why Power > Will Power

Whaaaaa???? Read. That. Again. Your *WHY* Power is GREATER THAN your *WILL* Power.

Let me break this down for you. How often do you hear someone say, "Man, if I had their willpower, I could do that too." News flash...Willpower is overrated! For example, I can say I need to have willpower and that I'm going to start working out and eating right. But the reality is, if I rely on my willpower, I'll probably hit snooze on my alarm tomorrow and skip the workout and by noon you'll find me in the Chick-fil-A drive-through. We've all been there, right?

However, if you know me, then you know I work out every day and eat right 90% of the time. Sounds like I have great willpower. But my will has nothing to do with my getting up at 5:30 a.m. and never skipping a workout. Nor does it keep me from eating fast food every day. But it has EVERYTHING to do with my *WHY* power.

Psst...here's my secret to living a healthy lifestyle. My father had a degenerative vein disorder that caused the vein grafts in his legs to shut down and ultimately led to his passing. This condition can be hereditary, and I have circulation issues already. But working out daily is preventative and lowers my risk for the same thing to happen to me.

I also have a stepdaughter who has to eat a restrictive diet. When we first found out how food was impacting her, I could tell she felt like it was an inconvenience, so I changed how I ate to make her feel included. That is my *why*. I'm so connected to those two things that I cannot compromise on them. My *Why* Power is what drives me to hold myself accountable to my workouts and eating habits. If there's something you want to accomplish and you don't know how to start, you MUST first dig deep to understand the *why* behind it. If you can tap into that, then girl, you can do anything.

You can have multiple *"whys."* A *why* for a healthy lifestyle, a *why* for a hobby, a *why* for your career. If you're sitting there reading this right now and you're like "I already know my *why*," stop right now. Let go of that preconceived idea. Take this journey with me. I'm not saying that you won't end up on the same *why*, but let's just reset for the purpose of the exercise. You may be surprised what you discover if you allow yourself a blank slate to really dig in and understand your true *why* power. But most importantly, you can discover and understand your "impact *why*."

Your impact *why* is centered on how you want to make an impact. Everything in your life can be narrowed down to this one word. In your core, it's the foundation of what motivates you. It's the imprint you want to make on this earth, on the people around you or as far as your reach allows. Understanding your impact *why* is the first step to living a brave life. But it takes digging deep and embracing your own story, your path for getting here.

Discovering this can be hard. Trust me. If you had asked me a year and a half ago, I wouldn't have known in the slightest what impact I wanted to make, and to be honest, I'm not even sure that I really cared. But you should care. We all have the ability to make an impact. And we should. We're here on this earth for a limited time. Why not live with purpose? We have one life—why are we not sprinting toward our wildest dreams like we're on fire?

It's important to understand too that sometimes impact and purpose don't have anything to do with others. It's about living a fulfilled life no matter how you live it. This is why understanding your impact why is so important. You don't have to invent something or come up with the cure for a disease to be a world changer. Although, if that's the impact you want to make, then yes, you should absolutely be relentless in pursuing those things.

But being a world changer can also be as simple as changing *your* world for the better. Happiness is a commodity. It's precious and should not be taken for granted because we've all learned at one point or another that it can be taken away in the blink of an eye. But sometimes pursuing our own happiness can feel self-centered.

Funny that often OUR happiness is tied to feeling guilty in some other aspect of our life. If you're a mother, you know exactly what this feels like. When you so desperately need a moment to yourself, away from your kids, just to feel happy and like a normal human again but you spend your whole time away feeling bad—for your kids and/or for your husband.

Or if you're not a mom, how many times have you done something you didn't want to do because you didn't want to disappoint someone else? These are all feelings driven from guilt—and it's a bunch of bolognas!!! (I gave you multiple this time because it was worthy of more than one.) I'm going to tell you a secret. In discovering your impact why, you can become free of the guilt that's tied to the sacrifices you have to make in order to truly be happy and here's why...

Your impact why is your super (why) power. Everything you do, every decision you make, every goal you set can be tied back to your impact why. Once you discover it and begin pursuing a life built around it, then you'll begin to make decisions based on it. And when something isn't in alignment with your why, you simply say "no thank you." Guilt free. Sounds too good to be true, right? But when you make a decision to live a (brave) life based on your why, you then give yourself permission to refuse anything in life that isn't centered on your why.

But before you can start refusing things that don't serve your why, you must first do the work to discover exactly what your impact why is. What is the very purpose behind why you want to make an impact for yourself or others? What gives you your passion? And what (specifically) motivates you to take action toward those things?

I thought I knew what my impact why was. I was so proud of myself too. (Besides, I'm the expert here, right?!? I mean I AM the one writing the book.) For the past year, I thought my why could all be tied back to one word...BRAVE. (I know, didn't see that one coming, did ya?) I mean if I had a dollar every time I used the word brave in the last year, I'd be giving this book away versus charging for it. I "brave" everything in life. Every day I use "brave" to propel me toward the life I want and the impact I want to make.

Women from all over know my mantra of "just braving it" and tell me how they did just that, braved it. Heck, my own children even use my own phrase back to me when faced with an uncomfortable situation... "You're just gonna have to brave it, Mom." So naturally, wouldn't "brave" be my one word to describe my impact why? I thought so. Until it hit me the other day in the shower. (This seems to be my place of epiphany moments so I'm sure you'll hear that again at some point in this book.) Brave is not your why, silly. Brave is your HOW. It's how you're living a life aligned with your impact why, but it isn't your why.

(MIND BLOWN)

> ***Spoiler Alert: I was able to identify my impact why, but I'm not going to share it just yet. That would be too easy. Let's take this journey together and I'll tell you mine after helping you to discover your own.***

Now, I'll get into creating a plan to live a brave life centered around your why and understanding the importance of being intentional about your "how" a little later in the book. But first, before you can do that, you have to discover YOUR impact why. And I may know a little something about this since I had to take this journey over the last few days to understand what it was for me.

Our impact why is unique to each of us. We may have similar purposes or desires. We may want to achieve similar things or make an impact for the same cause. We could even land on the exact same word to describe our impact why. But the *reason* we each have behind it is 100% all our own. We have all taken different paths to get exactly where we are today, in this moment. In many ways, our pasts always predict our futures. Decisions we make today, things we go through, things we accomplish, even moments where we fail, ultimately pivot us toward our future. No two stories are alike. But in understanding our own stories, looking at our own past helps us to understand not just who we are, but WHY we are.

There are two different types of stories to help us start to understand the "who" we are and the "why" that drives us to do what we do. These are what I like to call foundation and footer stories. In the next chapters we'll dig into each of these types of stories to help you become more intentional about your "who" and also, in understanding your who, help you discover your "why."

Reflect before you Neglect.

Write here:

If I could create the life I wanted without restrictions I would:

. . . .

. . . .

. . . .

My wildest, and I mean, wildest life dreams look like:

(Don't be getting all kinky on me. Keep it life fulfilling, not bedroom fulfilling.)

. . . .

. . . .

. . . .

What type of impact do I want to make? Individually or universally?

. . . .

. . . .

. . . .

throw a FREAKIN PARADE

CHAPTER TWO:

The Who

Nope, this isn't a chapter about the English rock band from the sixties. It's about the "Who" of you. "*Who*" are you? How many times have you asked yourself "Who am I?" We've all pondered this at multiple points of our lives. It's something we struggle with at times because, especially in today's day and time, understanding who we are, our unique identity, seems more important than ever.

How we are perceived, not just in life, but also in our virtual lives on social platforms seems to have become a priority that dictates a lot of the decisions we make. We can "create" a perception of any life we want and when we do, we wait to see how others respond—did I get enough views, comments, likes? And if we don't, we delete it...like it never happened at all, until we create another scenario (picture, video, post) that depicts another version of ourselves that we hope others will accept and like. It's pretty maddening, if you ask me. BUT I'm self-aware enough to know that I do the exact same thing. How many times do we check our social platforms AFTER we've posted something in comparison to days when we don't? We're looking to see who's watching, who's liking.

Social platforms have so much control over how we view others and ourselves. There was even a period of time that I got off all social platforms. Even in doing so, when I would tell others I wasn't on social media, it created a perception others had of me and one I also created for myself. (In my head it was that I was way too cool to be bothered by things like social media; that's what I told myself, and in some weird way it made me feel validated and cool.)

But why do we look to things like social media to validate our "who"? When that validation really has nothing to do with who we *actually* are. *Who* we are cannot be found on any social platform. No picture or perception of a life we post about tells anyone about the real "who" of you. And if you're looking there for validation or understanding of who you are or should be, then you're searching in the wrong place.

So then, where do we look to start to understand "Who we are"?

I think we overcomplicate the answer to this question more often than not. We all want to understand who we are, especially in moments when we feel lost. There is the "outward who," the person we project that we are, and the "inward who," the part of us that forms our opinions and thought patterns. The "outward who" is something we learn and create from others. From parents, friends, influencers, public figures, those we follow, and those we work with. We become who we project being from watching others and making our own assessments of the things we like and don't like about others.

When we see someone do something we like or find favor with, we'll often adapt a little of who we are to be a little like them— think style, mannerisms, things we say, and sometimes even things we say we believe (whether we do or not). And in the same breath, when we see things in others that we don't like, we tend to be purposeful in not acquiring those traits.

We can also tend to think that being a part of something or an environment—a friend group, a company, a position, or title within an industry—identifies us a particular way. This can also impact our "outward who" because when we identify with something, we tend to act a particular way to support that identity. But again, just because you're a part of something doesn't mean that's who you are.

When I was in youth group at church growing up, we had skits that we would perform on occasion for the church. My sister, best friend, and I wrote a skit that best describes exactly what this scenario looks like. We started by standing side by side dressed in black with our heads down. One of us raised her head slowly and said, "Where are we? Where are we?" and the other two would look around in amazement until one of us would say, "We're on a highway!" and the third would say excitedly, "That must make us cars!" and we would all run around the stage making car noises for thirty seconds until we reset and started all over...." "Where are we?" "McDonald's!" "That must make us a Happy Meal!" (Cue holding up hamburger, fries, and drink boards in front of us. (RESET) "Where are we?" "Church!" "That must make us Christians!" (Cue singing "Hallelujah" in our best operatic voices while we hold our hands in front of us like a formal choir) until one of us stops and says, "Wait, just because we're at church, it doesn't make us Christians—it takes accepting Christ, believing, and living the lifestyle."

Same is true of understanding who we are. Being a part of something doesn't make us who we are—it's our beliefs and how we live our lives that make us *who* we are. And how we live our lives has a lot to do with the lives we've already lived. This is the "inward who." How we were raised and the relationships we had with parents, friends, school peers, etc. all became a part of the "who" we've become. More specifically, the stories we remember with regard to the lives we've lived, with these individuals as lead roles, play the biggest part in not just who we are today, but who we want to become.

And when I say who we want to become, I am not talking about the perceived person we want people to think we are. I'm talking about the person we want to be as we live in our purpose in life. Reflecting on these stories, which I like to refer to as foundation stories, connects us to "who" we truly are.

Foundation Stories

Discovering what I like to refer to as "foundation stories" helps us identify not only more about who we are, but *why* we are who we are. A foundation story involves a period of time or event in your life that you remember in detail. More than likely, you've shared one with others to help them understand *why* you feel the way you do or respond to something a particular way. It's sometimes a story you tell on a first date or at a wine night with the girls. It can be the signature story you tell at new-hire lunches when getting to know new coworkers or the story you tell your teenage kids when they roll their eyes and say, "Ugh, why do you always...(insert annoying thing we do or say as a know-it-all parent here)?"

You feel emotion around it, connect to it, and can tell it like a memorized script. You draw conclusions in life as it relates to the way you make decisions, view things, or live today because of those stories. When we connect to our own foundation stories, we can better understand what drives us in our day to day. We understand our beliefs. We have opinions based on these stories. We connect with others because of these stories. Some are embarrassing, some give us bragging rights, and some share great loss.

Some foundation stories make us laugh, some make us proud, and some make us cry. But these stories help make us who we are. These stories can evolve and change as we live more life, thus also allowing our opinions and way of thinking to change.

Think in terms of a foundation on a home; when it's poured, it's a solid foundation that provides support for the walls built on it. But over time as the ground shifts and the environment around it changes, you may see cracks in it. The good news is these cracks can be filled, creating a stronger support for the home built on it. A foundation of a home can be seen at street level. It's a core part of the home. It may not be the most glamorous part (you don't invite someone to your new home and say "and just look at the level 5 foundation we had poured on this baby") but it's a part of every home and is imperative in understanding "why" and "how" the home is standing soundly.

You can add to a foundation when making additions to a home. Even if a storm were to come in and flatten the entire home, the foundation would still exist. It would take real work and heavy equipment to remove the foundation entirely and start over. (In life, we refer to this as years and years of therapy).

Your foundation stories serve you in the same way. These are the stories that can be seen by others because you share them and they're a core part of who you are. Everyone has their own foundation stories; understanding your foundation stories tell you, and others, who you are. It's important to understand who you are in order to understand your "why" and "how" to start living a brave life with purpose.

As you live, you may add to these stories or retire some altogether. But even in the hardest of times and in the seasons of storms in our lives, these stories still exist and often are what we hold onto to stay true to who we are when the world feels like it's crumbling around us. It's almost impossible to restart completely and change who we are as individuals, but years of therapy can help us to reset at times or see something differently.

We've all lived a lot of life. In fact, every moment up to this single one. So, defining which of your stories are your foundation stories may seem like a lofty task. But before settling on the ones that you think stand out the most, first think about some truths you know about who you are. These can be generalized truths to get you started. Things like I'm a perfectionist, or I'm OK with "good enough." I place value in my outer image, or I don't really care about superficial things. I need to control everything around me all the time, or I just like going with the flow. Once you do the work to identify your foundation stories, you'll then understand a little more about why these particular truths stand out most to you. Each of these truths connects to an event (foundation story) in your life that impacted your way of thinking and approach to life. In these truths is where you discover your "who."

Your "who" is the first factor in the equation of living a fulfilling life.

$$(who) + (\underline{\hspace{1.5cm}}) + (\underline{\hspace{1.5cm}}) = Fulfillment$$

We often fill our "who" with titles like mother, wife, sister, daughter, friend. Or even assistant, administrator, manager, director, VP. But none of those things is actually "who" we are. They're titles we or others give us. They may influence "who" we are, but they aren't the actual "who." All of those titles are about other people. You can't have a single one of those titles without someone else's involvement. When we define our who with titles such as those, then we allow what we are to other people to define "who" we are. That's not a true sense of "who." Your "who" is 100% about you.

Your "who" is not a title or what you are to someone else. Your "who" is YOU (insert name here) and all the wonderful (and sometimes not so wonderful) things that make up who you are. We need to stop defining ourselves by the value we bring to other people, because often other people let us down, or WE fail other people. And in both these scenarios, we often end up feeling lost.

When we identify our "who" based on who we really are vs. what we are to other people, then we never feel lost. Even when we fail ourselves or other people, it's just a failure, an opportunity to learn and grow, not a reason to feel lost or unsure of who we are.

Understanding your foundation stories and how they help to define your "who" makes you self-aware and gives you the ability to have more grace for yourself and your own quirks, and also, more grace for others and who they are. Some of my truths are that I believe to my core that God has a plan (and it's bigger than mine) and he will always provide. (That's nice.) I'm a perfectionist in its truest form. (Annoying.) I'm an overachiever with high achievement drive and thrive on accomplishment. (Yay, parade! Also annoying.) I love people, all people. (That's nice.) I'm curious by nature. (That's nice.) I enjoy material things but I don't take them for granted. (Annoying, but nice.) I've worked hard to get where I am today. (Nice.) I'm an advocate for women and have a deep calling to be a change leader. (OKKKK, niccceee, go get it, girl) So, why am I who I am? The next chapter will help explain a lot.

Reflect before you Neglect.

Write here:

What are some truths you know about yourself?

. . . .

. . . .

. . . .

. . . .

. . . .

. . . .

. . . .

. . . .

Your "who" is the first factor in the equation to living a fulfilling life. Write your name (not a title) in the equation below:

(_____) + (_____) + (_____) = Fulfillment
(who)

satisfaction guaranteed

OR YOUR

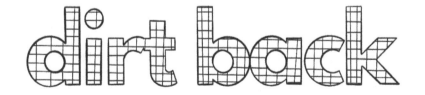

CHAPTER THREE:

Foundation Stories

Just a Small-Town Girl, Living in a....

I grew up in a small town in Alabama and was raised by parents who were magicians. Well, not technically magicians, but now as I look back as an adult, it would seem to be the case. They did a great job of shielding me from the adult struggles they dealt with while raising my sister, brother, and me.

My mother was a stay-at-home mom and made everything feel magical. She created special moments often and never made us feel like we went without, even though there were moments when we had to.

My dad was retired military. He worked full time at a country club while returning to school to get his degree at a local community college before going back to work for the Army in logistics as a civilian. He left work at the office and never spoke about it when he was at home. That amazes me when I think of how in today's world, work and home all bleed into one. He was a provider and worked hard but had the sweetest heart. I like to think that I got my work ethic from my father and my desire to create special moments for others from my mother.

I was a chatty child. (Let me guess, your facial expression didn't change when you read that sentence—no shock there, right?!?) My mom used to always say, "Amy will tell you her life story, and when she's done, she'll start all over." I loved talking to strangers (particularly the ones who drove white vans and offered me candy).

I was a curious child and had a true love for everyone, especially people who were different from me. (Note: I didn't own a white van and never had candy.) I had a unique ability and intuition, even at a young age, that could find commonality with almost everyone. It must be why I would talk people's ears off. I figured if I said enough, then eventually they'd stop me when they heard me say something they, too, had in common with me. I saw people as people; no one was better than me, and no one was worse. We were all the same.

I never thought much about material things back then. I thought about what I wanted but never about what I didn't have. What a gift. If only we could bottle childhood thinking for deposit later in life. Family life felt rooted in traditions and the special moments my mom created. I got along well with both my sister and my brother. I stayed out of trouble and did what I was told. I was a "good girl."

I had lots of childhood friends but one *best* friend, Becky. (Her parents drove a white van and the first time I met her in third grade she offered me candy—another non-shocker moment.) Our families became best friends. We attended the same church and our Friday nights consisted of Pizza Hut pizza, "Full House," and our mothers playing Scrabble at the kitchen table, our dads hanging out in the garage playing darts, and us kids playing "war" with the other neighborhood kids outside.

We lived in a modest ranch-style home at the end of a cul-de-sac in a town called Hartselle. It was walking distance to our elementary school, so we walked to school every morning because at that point my parents shared one car. I was never aware of how tight things were for us as a family when I was little. Sure, we didn't take vacations outside of driving to Michigan or Virginia to visit family. And on the rare occasion that we would eat out, I couldn't order the chicken nugget happy meal at McDonald's because it was "too expensive." But I was content and happy. I felt I had everything in the world that I needed. My parents were very loving and made sure we felt loved, safe, and provided for at all times. The reality was a lot of people had it better, and a lot of people had it worse; we had it just fine.

The Finer Things in Life (aka Underwear)

Our house seemed often to be the meeting point for all the neighborhood kids. I'm not sure why due to the fact that I was often giving the kids work to do. I have always been a big thinker and would often come up with some crazy ideas...that I couldn't do by myself. I was pretty persuasive even then and would convince everyone of the benefits of my ideas. On one particular hot summer day, when it would have been great to be inside an air-conditioned playroom or swimming in a creek somewhere, I came up with arguably the best idea I had in years...I mean days... I decided we were going to dig a hole to China off the side courtyard of my home under a dogwood tree.

Now before you write me off as crazy, let me explain. I'm pretty sure I told the other kids it was so we could all be famous and known as the first kids to dig all the way to China. But honestly, I just had an obsession with Hello Kitty and my hope was that we would dig directly under the Hello Kitty factory so I could get the Hello Kitty lunch box my mom told me was too expensive. I knew that it would be hard to rally all the other kids for this purpose; I'm not sure that the pink soft plastic lunch box with the zipper would have motivated them to spend their summer days digging for hours in my side yard. But "fame"? That would definitely motivate them to work for my cause. Seems kinda messed up looking back, but in my defense, it was one of the lunch boxes with the double layer plastic that had water and glitter in between and, y'all, it would have for certain made me the *most* envied girl at the lunch table.

So I felt totally justified in having my friends labor in the summer heat for me. For the record, I did bring them endless cups of cherry Kool-Aid. Also, for the record, I held two positions. I was what I like to refer to as the "Dig Supervisor" and a "Digger" (always an overachiever). In true Amy fashion, I had designated everyone dig shifts so we could be most productive. It was my little brother's turn to dig and as I sat in my chair watching him dig, I noticed something peeking from his waistline that looked familiar. I thought to myself, "Could it be? No, it can't be? Wait, I think it is...what the heck?" Is my brother wearing MY My Little

Pony underwear??? I yelled (with my Southern twang) "Roger Kent, are you wearing my underwear?" He sprang straight up and pulled his shirt down, then defensively and somewhat embarrassedly said back, "Yes, Mom made me wear them. I didn't have any that fit me anymore."

I was so confused; underwear was just something that you had. It's a necessity; everybody has underwear. So why was my brother wearing mine? I had no clue then that we, at times, did not have money for necessities like underwear.

Oddly enough, years later I heard my mom tell a story, as she spoke to a group of women at church, about a time when my sister and I did not have underwear that fit and in tears she prayed that God would provide means for underwear. The next day a neighbor knocked on the door and said she felt odd asking but that her daughter had gotten underwear for her birthday that didn't fit and could not be returned and she wanted to know if my mom could use them for us.

I learned three things from this:

> **One,** we struggled financially more than I was aware growing up.

Two, underwear is a luxury.

And three, God *always* provides.

Throw Me a Freaking Parade

When I was around 10, I overheard the tail end of a conversation that my mother was having with one of her friends where she said, "Amy is a mental child and she turned out OK." I spent the next few days confused about what that meant, even staring at myself in the mirror to see if I looked different from other people. I mean, I always was a little quirky, and I was self-aware enough even as a little girl to know it, but I wasn't sure what it meant to be mental. I remember thinking how impressed I was with family and friends that my whole life I thought I was completely ordinary because they did such a good job of not treating me different or letting on that I was "mental." It wasn't until later in the week that I was brave enough to ask my mom about it and she said, "Noooooo, I said middle. You are the middle child and you turned out OK."

Middle child, yes, that makes a lot more sense but in being the middle, "mental" wasn't too far off. There was additional stress I took on as the middle child that did weigh on my mental state. If you're a middle child, you can understand the need to create some sort of identity for yourself. My sister was the oldest—she got to do everything first. She was wiser, smarter, cooler. My brother was the youngest—forever the baby. And I, the middle.

We middle children go in several directions to create identities for ourselves. Some act out and become rebellious; others become introverts. Me? If I wasn't the oldest and wasn't the baby, then I would be "perfect." Or at least spend my time striving to appear to be. I made my bed every day. Wore matching hairbows and socks with every outfit. I vacuumed on the days when it wasn't my chore to do because no one else could do it as well as I could.

I became the epitome of a people-pleaser in its finest form. I began reading people at a very early age to figure out quickly what they wanted or needed in me and delivered every time. Disappointment was not in my vocabulary. I made it my life's work to be everything to everyone. I also recognized early on that in doing so I would be rewarded with praise and recognition. And I loved every single moment of it.

In elementary school, we were taught to put our heads on our desks when we were supposed to be quiet. I distinctly remember a moment in second grade in Mrs. Sandlin's class when a visitor came to the classroom to speak with her. The whole classroom began chatting and laughing among themselves while she spoke to the guest. I saw this as an opportunity to let my true self shine and I placed my head down on the desk and sat there quietly. Good girl, right?!? But in true Amy fashion, as the guest was leaving the room and before Mrs. Sandlin could address the class, I raised my hand and said, "Mrs. Sandlin, look at me, I'm being good." This was me to a T. I was going to do it, and do it right, but I was dang sure going to get credit for it! Still to this day, I'm that way. I'm going to do it, and I'm going to do it right, but I dang sure need a parade when I do! (Hey—at least I am self-aware.)

Perfection as a little girl felt more like hope. It felt attainable, or at least the appearance of perfection felt so. My mother's love for me was so evident. She seemed to beam when talking about me and my matching hair bows and socks. In my small world I found happiness in those moments. Don't get me wrong; my mother knew I wasn't perfect, but my desire to please her and my father was. My striving for perfection in the way I looked, things I did, and desire to get it right every time was evident. So, in the moments when I wasn't perfect, I learned quickly how to shift and move to create the appearance of perfection. This became an art that I carried with me into adulthood. The idea of perfection seemed like an ideal goal, whether it was to be perfect for my parents, my teachers or frankly anyone who was paying attention. In case you are unaware, perfectionism takes a ton of energy to strive for. That may be great when you're eight and have enough energy to light up lower Manhattan, but when you're 44, perfectionism is exhausting!

What I've come to recognize is that this need for perfection can become a toxic trait as we become adults for two different reasons.

1. It can be hard to be brave when we're constantly seeking perfection because of fear of failure. This fear can keep us from taking big risks because we like to stay within the boundaries where we know we can succeed versus pushing outside our comfort zones and tackling bigger risks.

2. Striving for perfection can also cause what I like to refer to as hanging carrot syndrome. We become so focused on the superficial, tangible things like awards, titles, and accomplishments that even though we celebrate in the moment (and believe me, I ride that parade float waving the whole way), once the moment passes, we're left empty

searching for the next thing and can never truly be content or satisfied.

Shifting your mindset on this can be difficult. But if you can align yourself with your purpose and become more focused on building your legacy rather than your resume, you'll begin to find fulfillment from the work you're doing to better the lives around you versus your own.

It doesn't mean that there are no longer parades thrown in your honor in the future. Trust me, I still throw myself a good ole parade on the weekly. I fully believe in and embrace celebrating our wins. But perfection is built on an idea that is rooted in self-centeredness. The only way to break the pattern of need for perfection is to shift your thinking from a place that is centered on you and move toward a place that is centered on others.

Start looking for reasons to throw other people a parade. You can still wave; you might just be driving the float rather than sitting on top of it. As individuals, we should be looking for opportunities to pour into other people's cups. Now, I can't completely fill someone else's cup. But I can empty some of mine into others'.

I refer to this in leadership as a "Hereafter" Leader. So "here" being in the today, while understanding the "after" is what today's work will leave for the next generation of leaders who will come behind you. When we look back at the end of our lives and careers, will we be able to say we left our companies and industries better because of the lives we touched? Not that we were perfect, but we were authentic. Not what we achieved, but how we celebrated others' achievements. Not what we were recognized for, but how we took the time to recognize others.

(But just keepin' it real and authentic, I still love a good ole Amy Druhot Parade)

Idaho? No, Udaho

Growing up my family spent a lot of time at church. And by "a lot" I mean, every Sunday morning, Sunday night, and Wednesday night. I loved it, in fact I lived for vacation Bible school and church camps. Faith was always deeply rooted in who I am as a person. I remember my junior year of high school, I attended a youth camp and we did an exercise about writing our testimony. I really struggled because I felt up until that moment my life had been mild. Remember, I was *reeeeally* good at *"appearing to be"* perfect. What could my testimony be? *"Hey, guys, I'm Amy and when I was born, God threw himself a parade in honor of his creation of perfection. Come to the altar and cast out those demons of imperfection and be perfect like me."* Not sure I would have brought many to Christ that way. However, about a year later God must have been tired of my complaining about not having a testimony and turned to Jesus and said, "Hold my beer. (We'll get to that later.)

But overall, I am and was a good girl. Stayed out of trouble. I don't cuss. I tend to use words like fudge, dang, or my personal favorite "ish." As in... "Well, ain't that some ish!"

Side note: If you want a lesson in effective communication, this is it: Never cuss... And tell people you don't cuss. *Completely* embody your non-cussing self on the daily...and then...when you need to effectively communicate, and the other person isn't listening, strategically drop the F bomb. Ever seen someone's eyeballs pop out of their head and get the full-on body sweats and shake from head to toe while their head spins? Yep, that's what I refer to as "effectively communicated."

Anyways, I only drank once before I turned 21. Never went to parties or tried any drugs—not even a cigarette. But, girl, bless my heart, I was a ho.

I'm just kidding, I wasn't a ho...

(Yes I was.)

Totally kidding, I wasn't.

(Oh, I definitely was)

Was not.

(*Wink, wink.*)

In all seriousness, I hoped on waiting until marriage. And, as we all know, hope is not a strategy. At the age of 20, I found myself pregnant with my first son. His father wanted to flip a coin...heads we keep him, tails we didn't. (True story.) But also, true story...it was never a question for me. I wasn't living the lifestyle of most 20-year-olds, so I didn't feel I was going to miss out on much. As scared as I was, I fell completely in love with his little life the moment I found out I was pregnant. This was my first real "just brave it" moment. What would my parents think? My friends? My church? I remember feeling embarrassed, alone, and afraid. But also, with a feeling of more purpose than I had ever felt. BUT, no parade this time. Perfect image—out the window. Self-centered ways—out the door. Ideas of what I thought life would look like—out with the trash. Whole life pivot moment. His father disappeared and became distant.

About three months in, I made a phone call to him and said, "I wouldn't stay with you if you were treating me this way and I wasn't pregnant, so I'm not going to stay with you just because I am. (Just brave it moment number two.) Not only was I going to do this; I was going to do it alone. Don't get me wrong; my parents were amazing and so supportive. Friends were great and even excited, but time spent with them lessened. Let's face it, hanging out with my pregnant belly didn't help with their dating lives. Church was awkward, like super, super awkward. But I wasn't cast out or anything. I just remember feeling an immense amount of shame as people stared and whispered.

Speeeeaking of awkward and shame...SIDE STORY. (Disclaimer: If you're a man reading this book, you're welcome to skip this one. Or at least don't say I didn't warn you. Or if you're a young woman, get ready to learn something they never tell you before having kids.) As if I wasn't already ashamed enough—young, pregnant, out of wedlock—my pastor, being supportive, decided to visit me in the hospital after I had Brayden. Now, what they don't tell you after you have a baby is that you don't have total control of all your bodily functions right after you give birth. You also don't have any control of the timing of those odd bodily functions. And you're also pretty numb, so you don't even really know what's happening when it happens. So, my pastor walked in and I went to adjust myself in the bed to sit up a little higher and I must have had an air bubble trapped somewhere that my body decided to release in that exact moment. Y'all, it was loud, like the start of the Hallelujah Chorus loud, and I'm not even sure what part of my body it came from. But, in front of my pastor?!?! Seriously, God?!? He tried to ignore it and started talking really loud, but I think he didn't know if he should congratulate me or cast out the deep-voiced demon screaming from beneath my hospital sheets. Not sure if that was one of God's "hold my beer" moments or what part of my testimony that was supposed to shape into, but lawd, it sure didn't help on the awkward and shameful scale as it related to attending church.

But becoming a young single mother was the best thing that had ever happened to me. That sweet precious boy changed my life. I remember watching him all night long the first night of his life, his little chest rising and falling. I felt responsible for making sure he took every single little breath. I was terrified he would stop breathing. And I remember in that moment realizing that life wasn't just about me. That I was going to do everything

I could to provide for him and protect him. That I needed to be more than I was before him. "Me" was now a "We" and life would never be the same.

It was then that I started to "work with purpose." I had a reason outside of myself to show up every day. But not just show up, grow up. I don't mean in maturity or age. Show up and grow up meant that I needed to position myself for growth and opportunity. Because the gravity of my work and the stability the work provided intensified.

When we work with purpose, we show up differently in the work that we're contributing to and expect to grow up into the future opportunities we hope to seek to provide a better life. The "who" I was was now a mom. But I'm not saying you have to have a child in order to work with purpose. You just have to understand where your motivation comes from and the why behind it.

I can't tell you how many times in my career I've watched young women become mothers; it transforms them as employees. But not in a way that many would expect. Because I also can't tell you the number of times I've heard people, unfortunately primarily men, say, "Well, that's the end of her career. She's becoming a mother so she'll be unmotivated, distracted, distant." Bo-log-na!!! (Oh, my word, y'all—I just asked Siri how to spell bologna and realized it's ACTUALLY spelled baloney for the purpose of how I've been saying it! I like the other better so I'm leaving it—authentic, not perfect, right?!?)

Some of the best career transformations I've seen have been when women who've worked for me come back from maternity leave. Some get borderline downright ruthless! Just think, when you become a mother, nothing is more important than the life you're now responsible for. So, if you have to be away from your child for 40+ hours a week, you're going to dang sure make it worth your while.

So, in your current "who," what is your show up and grow up thing that gives you the ability to work with purpose? At 20 it was my son, at 35 it was to prove something, and at 44 it's being a "hereafter leader." Each of the phases of my life clearly defined my "who" and they were rooted in the stories before and during them.

Etsy High School

My background was not a traditional one for someone who ends up in a vice president of sales role. Like, AT ALL. I dropped out of high school a few months before completion due to what started as a normal breakup with a guy that escalated into a group of girls (one of whom was now dating the guy) who were relentless about trying to make me feel horrible about myself. They would heckle me, throw water bottles at me in the parking lot, write my name (and some not so nice things) on the bathroom wall, make up rumors, laugh loudly as I walked by. I was an easy target because I didn't fight back, kept my head down, and was even nice to them and allowed them to use me for rides, thinking they wanted to become friends despite the roller coaster of befriending and betrayal. My mom was fed up with the tears and allowed me to pull out of school. I did some homeschooling curriculum to finish, I think, but was never really sure if I actually graduated. A few years back I asked my mom because I never actually got a diploma. So she ordered me one, on Etsy, and gave it to me in 2019. Not kidding. Here it is:

It was one of the best gifts I've ever received. Not because it confirmed I graduated from high school—that's still debatable—not sure Etsy is qualified to distinguish that honor. But because it was thoughtful and a gift from my mom to provide some sort of closure. I'm not sure it did that, but if nothing else, it did provide a good laugh. And also, it reminded me that it didn't matter. Don't get me wrong; I highly respect education and the need for it. But having or not having a high school diploma did not make me a good single mother, or resilient in times when I had no choice but to pivot, or help me knock it out of the park when I went in to an interview for a job I had no experience in or qualifications for.

But what it did do was make me realize that nothing was owed or guaranteed to me because I did or didn't have one. That at the end of the day it was up to me to show up, learn (grow up), and work hard...show up, learn (grow up), and work hard. That the value of the belief I had in myself and my drive to want to prove I was worthy and capable outweighed a diploma, or lack thereof.

Collections, New Homes, or a Glitter Stripper Pole
Cue problem number one—uhhhh, last I checked most jobs require a high school diploma or GED—at least the real adult jobs, right?!? And no chance to go to college without one, so how was I going to make a life for myself? Lucky for me, a large credit card company had a campus nearby and they needed collection agents. My sister worked there and could put in a referral. They were in the process of hiring 160 agents, so with the referral and their need to bulk hire, I applied and somehow landed the job!

I felt like I hit the lottery! Set pay, full benefits, full time schedule AND bonus opportunity based on performance!?! (Remember, I love a carrot and the cause for a parade!!) Your girl got in there and lit that place up. Promoted from early to late stage to temporary floor supervisor and then high balance accounts.

(Rich people collections—yep, there is such a thing as being rich and still forgetting to pay your bills.)

By this time, I was now married to my second son's father, with three children at home (my "step"-daughter Jade, my son Brayden, and my baby Kobe. "Step" is nonsense; she's my daughter.) The company was outsourcing these roles and laying off internally. My then husband also worked at the same company, so we made a decision that one of us would need to seek other employment so we didn't have all our eggs in one basket in case there were layoffs. I saw an ad for a customer service administrative role for a well-known national new home construction builder and applied.

Lucky for me, our market looked kindly on individuals who had experience working for this bank in our market. Who better to handle customer service concerns from upset homeowners than someone who had been calling people at 8 a.m. on a Sunday morning to collect a debt? I'd grown a VERY thick skin. I'll never forget the phone call when the office manager, Joy, called me and offered me the job. She told me that when the leadership team met after I interviewed, they all said they were "enamored" with me. I had never even heard the word before and didn't know what that meant but I was elated. (Someone with an actual high school diploma would have probably known what they meant.)

This is where I fell in love with the new homes industry. It wasn't always easy—I was on the receiving end of unhappy people calling in for service on their homes. And trust me, if you want to hear some upset people, deal with someone whose roof is leaking on the home they just closed on. People get crazy over that stuff. I was eventually promoted to settlement administrator and worked on the closing side. We were making people's dream homes a reality; it was a great industry to be in. Um, until it wasn't.

Cue problem number two, the recession. On the third round of layoffs, I was called into the office and told I was being let go. I was and wasn't surprised. I did a good job, but I was goofy as all get out. I don't know that the individuals who worked with me during that time would have ever thought that I would have ended up being as successful as I have become. During my exit interview I was told by my sweet office manager that of all the people they were having to let go, I was the one that they were least worried about because of my creativity.

"Maybe you'll be a children's book writer or something like that; you're just so creative." To which the division president at the time added, "Or you could be a dancer." Yep...that's what he said as the office manager's jaw dropped. For the record, I've never taken a single class of ballet or tap in my life so we all know what he meant. It was an inspiring day, to say the least.

I remember going home that day and crying. My son Kobe, then 5 years old, wrapped his arms around me and told me he loved me and said it would be OK after telling him I just wanted my job back. Wise little soul. Why would I want to go back to something where after four years of contributing to a company, the only words of advice the DP had for me was that if all else failed, I could be a dancer?...Stability.

Stability is a good thing, right? It's our human nature to desire and value stability. Safety, structure, routine, security. But the problem with stability is that we tend to overvalue and prioritize it to a point where it's no longer a good thing. Take, for example, how many of you reading this book have ever stayed in a relationship too gosh darn dang long? Or know someone who has? All of us, right? And why? It's because we're overvaluing stability. Something that once was good. But over time, a stability-seeking strategy can hurt us. Because when we're seeking stability over stepping outside our comfort zones, a day turns into a month, which turns into a year and then it's three years and we're looking back saying, "What the heck?"

How did I stay in a relationship so long that wasn't serving me. People will often think it's out of fear, but it's not. It's that we overvalue stability. The devil we know is better than the one we don't. So if we're prioritizing stability, or a paycheck, or a title, or routine, or whatever it may be, then we'll be paralyzed and not moving toward what would bring us fulfillment. We must step out of a place of prioritizing stability and start moving toward fulfillment if we want to live a brave life.

I was crying over the loss of stability. But, even though at the time I didn't know it, it was a step toward finding fulfillment. That layoff would be one of the best things that ever happened to me in my career.

Satisfaction Guaranteed or Your Dirt Back

The recession was weird. I was back in the job pool, and it was tiny...better described as the "baby pool." Shallow, small, and if you did find a job floating in there it was a good chance it was crap. (I just made myself giggle on that one.)

But it was true. I was going out for interviews, and competing with people who had MBAs who were desperate for a job, and getting offers for $10–15K less than what I had been making prior. I just didn't want to take a step back. This was easy to say but when you have a family that you need to contribute to supporting, it's another story. Not wanting to live off unemployment and getting discouraged by the offers and lack of possibilities, I decided that I had to do something to support my family, so I started my one-woman-show cleaning business.

"Pick Me Up Cleaning Services." Because everyone could use a pick me up—especially me at that point in my life. My slogan was "Satisfaction guaranteed or your dirt back!" And I'm very proud to say that in four years of cleaning, not one person asked for their dirt back! I made flyers and drove from neighborhood to neighborhood putting them in mailboxes. I told friends and family members. I even ended up cleaning my dentist and his wife's house; he was very successful...and also, an ex-boyfriend. I think the first time I cleaned their house I was there for almost eight hours. I figured if all I ever amounted to was being a house cleaner, then I was going to be the best dang house cleaner he'd ever seen.

It was good hard work; I built up a full two-week schedule. I also got to put my kids off and on the bus each day, so I was able to be more present for my kids during those years. I'm so grateful for that. But I'm also grateful for the perspective it gave me: the respect I now have for anyone doing any job. It was hard work. Even in my early 30s I'd go home with my legs and back aching most days. And don't get me started about when I'd run into someone I knew who would ask what I was doing and I had to say I was cleaning houses.

Over time, I realized that the work I was doing was good work. It made the lives of the people I was cleaning for better, and I was good at it. Most importantly, I was providing for my family. I was proud of that. To this day there isn't a toilet I wouldn't roll up my sleeves to clean if the owner of my now company was coming to town and it needed to be done. There's no work that one person is responsible for doing that is beneath another. We're all doing the best we can and we should all respect each other for that.

It's hard to believe that that was just 13 years ago. I feel like a completely different person than who that Amy was. But I wish I could go back to her now in the times when she thought that was all there was for her to tell her that she would be so much more. That she would work her way back and exceed all her expectations. I think that's why today a lot of "who" I am is an encourager of women. Because I want to see every woman around me reach her full potential. And not just watch, but help show them how and let them know that I believe they can.

Smoke and (Glass) Mirrors

The market started to correct, and I found a job with a commercial construction company. It got me back into the employment world with good pay but didn't give me fulfillment. I would check the classifieds weekly and apply whenever I saw something different that piqued my interest. I had moved through the interview process with a video integration company for an accounts payable role (wow, how my life would have been different) and received a job offer I was about to accept. I was still getting job notifications via email and the evening that I accepted the AP role, I saw an ad for a marketing manager for a local home builder.

When I was a teenager, a job in marketing was my dream job. I had always been creative (thus my cleaning slogan) BUT I had absolutely no experience. I almost deleted the email with the job post, then stopped and thought... "What's the worst that can happen? SO, I never hear from them? It's at least worth a try." (Just brave it, right?!?) So, I applied. Much to my surprise, the

VERY next day I had just come in from a run and was checking my email when I received a message from the hiring manager.

He said he'd received my resume on LinkedIn and wanted to speak with me regarding opportunities with his company. This was a little odd because I didn't actually have a LinkedIn... BUT I didn't care—this was my dream job and they actually wanted to speak with me! All I had to do was sell myself!

The following Friday I went in for my interview. The hiring manager seemed a little off but overall we had great conversations. He even said that if I wasn't a match for that role, he would find another role within the company. So I was feeling pretty confident about the possibility of working there. A few days later he called and offered me the job.

I couldn't believe that I had landed the one job that, if I had gone to college, would have been what I wanted to do for a living. He also told me that the reason he seemed off was because he actually did not mean to email me when he originally reached out. (That explains the LinkedIn comment.) He meant to email someone else and didn't realize it until the morning of my interview when he printed off my resume. WOW...OK, God, I see what you did there.

I remember where I was when we had that conversation. And I remember his exact words. He said, "It may sound like **smoke and mirrors**, but I truly feel like all of this happened for a reason." (He did also reach out to the person whom he meant to email and interviewed her as well. I believe he offered her the job first because of her experience but she turned it down.)

So there I was accepting my dream job. From cleaning houses to marketing them. I was so excited for the future.

Smoke and mirrors is a phrase regarding magicians using smoke to obscure their movements and mirrors to create illusions, making their tricks more baffling to the audience. We now use it as a blanket phrase to describe anyone or anything that's not truthful. The irony of this as it relates to this individual is uncanny. But that is a story for another day.

I led the marketing efforts for two years before being promoted to sales manager. (With no prior sales experience!) I was breaking through glass ceilings that I never thought would even be in my vision. I tackled that opportunity, as I have everything else in life—with all I had. I didn't know the sales side, but I knew the heart side. The people business. That's what the role of a sales leader truly is.

So, I did just that. Lead with my heart—show up and grow up—that's what I did every day. Every day until the environment was no longer good for me. I stayed longer than I should have—dang stability. I was overvaluing the stability of the paycheck (I was making more money than I'd ever hoped for) and the title (I was in a role I had no qualifications for). But I was eventually brave enough to make a step toward seeking out true fulfillment and made the decision to leave...Another "Just Brave It" moment that would also be one of the best decisions I've made in my career.

A couple years back, I was in a company leadership training and the individual leading the discussion said, "You're all in this room right now because someone, at some point, saw something in you that they felt was worthwhile investing in." I immediately knew who that person was for me. Because if he hadn't taken a chance on me, I wouldn't be where I am right now. And, although the relationship has since been severed, I know I owe him some gratitude for that start.

It's a Man's World, but it would be nothing without...
When I left there, my imposter syndrome was higher than it had ever been. Was I actually good at my job or was I given the

position for other reasons? I was told I would be given the VP of sales role but I needed to "act" like the job I wanted. What did that even mean?

The only people I knew in the position prior were men. Don't dare to be yourself. Dress the part, act the part. So I was doing all that. I didn't even realize to what extent. I remember one of the other women who worked there gave me feedback that she didn't feel I was authentic. I was so bothered by this and thought she was wrong. But she wasn't. (Katy, you weren't wrong.) I was constantly trying to be what I thought others expected of me and who I thought I needed to be to get to the next promotion. I wasn't being myself.

2017 was a good year, despite leaving that job. I received the Sales Manager of the Year award for my market for the 2016 year. I built a home. I got engaged, and not just engaged, but I got to plan and have the engagement and wedding I didn't have in my early 20's. Complete with engagement parties, girls' weekends, and a wedding with 160 in attendance. My children were all thriving. The blending of the two families went without a bump. Our combined 7 children all loved each other and got along without a hitch! (If you have a blended family, you know how difficult this can be.) Holidays with the new family dynamics were magical. AND your girl finally got enough balls to step away from stability.

That, in itself, is empowering. To just brave it and leave something based on principle even though you don't know what's next. It's scary, but it was right. I chose to lean in and trust God— if he can provide underwear, he can provide a job.

In less than two weeks after leaving I started with a lending and real estate firm as the director of real estate. This was what I like to refer to as a "stepping stone job." It was a job. It provided for my family. It gave me the confidence to step away from a toxic environment. But by the end of the first week, I knew it wasn't going to bring fulfillment.

"Job hopping" is something that people tend to tie a negative connotation to. We need to stop doing this. Talk about overvaluing something that we shouldn't. We should applaud individuals who get to work to provide for their families but have grown professionally enough to quickly identify the environments that aren't right for them.

Now, if you job hop over and over, at some point you have to look in the mirror and ask yourself if it's a "you" problem and determine what it is you're actually searching for. But if someone leaves an environment that no longer serves them and goes to another that also doesn't serve them, why do we as a society expect them to stay? If we stay for appearances because we're worried that we'll be labeled as a job hopper, then we're overvaluing what we're mistaking as commitment instead of fulfillment. And in this scenario, nobody wins. Not the employer, who's investing time and money in a person who isn't the right fit. Not the employee, who's wasting time and energy giving to something that doesn't fulfill them.

So, let's start valuing individuals who are aware enough to identify this early and move on for the sake of all who are involved. It's not a commitment problem. They are committed—to being brave enough to seek out their own fulfillment.

When I announced that I was leaving the builder whom I worked for, I immediately received an email from an old friend I'd worked with back at the national builder when we were both just starting our careers. He was now the market manager for another builder who was new(er) to our market, and he had seen my successes as a sales leader. He said he was going to start the process of looking for a sales manager and was wondering what I was going to be doing next. My first response was that I was going to step away from new homes and because I loved my old team so much, I didn't want to sell against them.

But the truth was, I was doubting my sales leadership capabilities. Even though my team at my last company was knocking it out of the park and my sales efforts were being acknowledged on a market level, the individual I reported to had done a number on my confidence because he "wasn't getting his way." (Remember, the impostor syndrome was real at this point.) So even though I was brave enough to step away, and I did a good job of "braving it until I made it," I was broken and confused.

Now, remember how I referred to the new job as a stepping stone? Well, these stones were anything but smooth. I couldn't hop across those babies fast enough. So, at the end of that first week, I emailed my friend back with a "How about that lunch?"

Thank God I did. That lunch turned into an offer, which turned into an opportunity with an amazing culture- and value-rich company. And not because they throw mission words on a wall in the office or hold classes to teach the values. You see, when the culture and values are real and authentic and start from the top down, you don't have to invest thousands of dollars shoving them down the throats of your employees. They just exist; they are lived. In the work being done and in the heart and actions of those doing the work.

When I met the owner of the company for the first time, I was trying to impress him with my industry knowledge and ability to convert sales, as we all do in an interview. He listened respectfully and intently and when I stopped, he said, "Wow, Amy, that's all fantastic. But at Eastwood we believe that if you do the right thing, and you treat people the right way, the results will come." I was sold.

Go find you a company that not just says that but believes it. I was lucky enough to find this. If you're the owner of the company and want to have a culture rich in values and respect, look inward first. I will never understand organizations who have outside companies come in and define and teach your values. Where is the authenticity in that?!? (Especially when the leadership is corrupt and they're doing it just to make themselves "look" good—phony bolognas!)

For once, I felt seen, heard, and trusted. Didn't matter what my educational background was or my path to get there. Didn't matter what gender I was or how I looked and acted. Everything about who I was and what got me to that moment was (and is) celebrated. When you report to someone who's kind and wants to see those around them succeed, it's amazing the magic that can come out of that. Everyone is given the autonomy and support to make their own path to success. It's a beautiful thing. It aligned with the way that I lead—with the heart.

The performance of my team grew. We all were showing up and growing up—and still do to this day. (Can you tell I love my job?) Over six years, I was promoted from sales manager to sales director and last year vice president of sales. I was giving and investing a lot, and they saw that, celebrated it, and gave it back.

It took me almost 20 years in a career to feel like I was actually seen. That's awful. I was growing up and showing up the whole time—20 years—but never felt 100% truly seen. And why? I'd like to say that it was because I'm in a male-dominated industry and we're evolving. We've made progress, but we aren't there. I mean, today there's no way you could get away with telling someone when laying them off that they could "be a dancer."

But just because it's (hopefully) not being said, have the mindsets of those individuals actually shifted?

But worse than that, the men were not the only issue. The women I encountered at times throughout my career were sometimes just as bad. We've all been there, right?! The amount of cattiness, competition, and downright mean girl mentality that I've seen or experienced in my career is heartbreaking. But it doesn't have to be that way.

We should be celebrating each other and supporting one another. There's nothing better than a band of women with a collective intention coming together to support one another.

This weighed on me. I was truly "working with purpose," but I felt conflicted. If it took me 20 years to find a place of feeling seen, then I couldn't be the only one. Where were the female mentors and supporters throughout my career? Don't get me wrong; I worked with some amazing women through the years. But where was the intentionality of support, direction, and even at times, protection? It was every woman for herself. I knew in my heart it didn't have to be that way. It doesn't have to be that way.

Working for a company that trusts and supports me, not just in my daily work but also in the way that I want to give back to this industry, is invaluable. I always lead my team with heart and become invested in each individual, man or woman, in a way that I wish I would've had someone invest in me.

So when my heart kept pulling toward the work needing to be done on a larger scale, I knew that I had a purpose and calling that was bigger than the work of just a sales leader. That true fulfillment for me was becoming both a sales leader and a change leader.

I encouraged my good friend, who's well known on a national level, to create a space for women through an all-female national women's leadership circle. I love that she called it a circle because although I encouraged her to start it, participating in it is what actually encouraged me to be brave enough to start advocating for women in my market and ultimately to write this book. So, full circle moment. And I truly believe that my work is just getting started.

Who even is Amy Druhot?

These are just a few of my foundation stories. But they reveal so much about the "who" that "Amy" is. Believer. Perfectionist. Lover of all. Parade thrower. Advocate. Change leader.

Glitter, Glitter, Dirt, Dirt, Glass and Fart.

Connecting to your foundation stories can help you better understand who you are. However, as much as a foundation story connects you to who you are, it isn't what makes you brave or fulfilled.

Brave is described as an adjective, but when you live a brave life, it becomes a verb. It's an action. It's what moves you out of where you are and into where you want to be—living a life of fulfillment. Brave requires grit. It doesn't mean that you're fearless. It means that in the moments when you're afraid, you act anyway. Just as understanding your "who" is important, finding your *why* is also key to living a brave life of fulfillment . But to discover your why, you must go deeper—to your "footer stories."

Reflect before you Neglect.

Write here:

Thinking about the truths you wrote that you knew about yourself at the end of the last chapter, what foundation stories can you connect to the "Who" you are today?

....

....

....

....

....

....

....

....

....

....

glitter glitter

DIRT
DIRT

GLASS &

Fart

CHAPTER FOUR:

The Why

Why. A word based in curiosity and confirmation. It's the word we use when we're seeking to understand. If you look up the definition of the word, it says it's the "cause, reason or *purpose for which.*" **Purpose**. I love that. Because in the sense of how it's written in the definition, it's really relating to the purpose of why something was or is done a particular way. But as it relates to us as individuals, our *why* is our *purpose*. Specifically, our Impact Why.

Your "impact why" is the second factor in the equation of living a fulfilling life.

(who) + (why) + (_____) = Fulfillment

Remember earlier when we talked about our Why Power being greater than our Will Power? When we get connected to our why, we're living (and working) in our purpose, and we're not willing to compromise on that. But first, how do we discover our why?

As I mentioned earlier, we can have lots of "whys" for things. The multitude or "generalized why" is a strategy many of us use to help get us up and motivated for the day. It's a "hope strategy" that if I generalize to myself that my children are my why for *everything I do,* then I'll be more committed in my day to day because everything I do is for them. I mean, that's nice and all but is it truly helping you to level up your life?

I believe these "generalized whys" can be effective in moments of despair. Ask a momma who's about to lose her house and is struggling to put food on the table why she's working three jobs and only sleeping three hours a day. I can guarantee that she'll show you a picture of her children. But in that scenario, she's using her why for survival, not purpose.

The reason a generalized why doesn't work as it relates to purpose is because it's just that, general. It's too widespread. Think of your why as the "icing on the cake" as it relates to your life. It's the finishing touch, what makes you complete. A generalized why is the Betty Crocker Vanilla Sprinkle tub icing...y'all already know where I'm going with this, right?!? Why Betty Crocker would sell you a tub of icing that simply will not cover the whole cake is beyond me. And forget about icing the middle layer. No matter how thin your spread it, it just won't cover it.

That's how a generalized why works. It may be there, but there's no way it can cover all aspects in life and can leave some areas exposed altogether. How are you supposed to live a brave life that feels completely fulfilled (covered) when you're generalizing your why behind it? It may exist, but it's not specific enough to fulfill us.

If you want to cover the whole cake, you're going to have to start from scratch. Homemade. Which requires more work. But the work you put in also allows you to be measured in each step to make sure that you're covered and filled (and if you're lucky, you might even get to lick the bowl).

That's why it's important to understand your *impact why* vs. having a generalized why. Your impact why makes up your purpose. It's the main ingredient in leveling up your life. It's specific. And the good news is it already exists within us. Much like understanding who we are, our impact why is made up of our past stories and experiences that have helped to form our opinions and motivations in life. Homemade. But instead of focusing on our foundation stories to discover this, we need to focus on our footer stories.

Footer Stories

In new construction, footers are found under the foundation. Footers can't be seen, but they're there, under it all. They go deeper than the foundation and are critical. They ensure that the structure doesn't sink into the ground by distributing the weight evenly across a larger footprint. Much like the icing example, footers have all structural aspects of the home sitting on top of them covered. So that not just the foundation, but the structure built on top of that foundation is sound and able to effectively serve its purpose.

Our footer stories serve the same purpose for our lives. These are the stories and experiences that we hold deep within us that form the why behind what we do and what pull us out of complacency and into purpose.

A great example of this is the nonprofit industry. If you look to the start of most of these organizations there was a trigger moment, a story, an experience that moved someone out of the life they were previously living and into a life built on purpose. Their lives were impacted in some way that caused them to apply, what I like to refer to as, the "Missy Elliott Technique." They had a life they were living, then something happened that caused them to "put that thing down, flip it, and reverse it."

They were impacted by a loss, a disease, hunger, etc., so now they're abandoning their old life (putting that life down), reevaluating it (flipping it), and committing to wanting to create a solution or support for others who have been impacted in the same way (reversing it).

I believe if you were able to interview the founders of most of these organizations, they would say that they're now living more purposeful lives, despite what they had to go through to get to this new life. It's not because their lives didn't have trauma. It's because they did, but then they took that trauma and turned it into purpose. They were impacted (negative) and now want to make an impact (positive).

The key here is the word impact. Something impacts us that then predicts how we want to impact. The same goes when defining your impact why. You may not have been impacted by a traumatic loss to this point in your life but that doesn't mean that the life you've lived can't help you define what would bring you more fulfillment and purpose.

Finding your impact why doesn't mean that you need to abandon your current life to become a scientist, non-profit founder, or the next world change leader. It's about defining the impact you want to make. In *the* world, or *just in your* world. It doesn't matter how big or small. It could just be the impact you want to make for your own life to find more happiness and fulfillment in the life you're already living. Understanding this can help us level up how we parent, how we work, or who we invest in. It can help us find direction for a larger purpose.

It also gives us permission to set boundaries. To say no when something doesn't align with our purpose and to go all in when it does. It gives us back margin in our lives, so we have more capacity for the things that make us happy. We can finally stop overcommitting and over showing up for others when we're struggling to show up for ourselves. We all want that, right?!? Wait, scratch that...we all NEED that, am I right?!?

Our impact why holds us accountable to living a brave life based on our purpose. Remember, when we discover our "why power," we will not compromise. We have no choice to be brave because when something doesn't align with our (impact) why, we respond appropriately to stay within our purpose.

Unlike our foundation stories, discovering our footer stories can be tough. Not because they're not as easily discovered. In fact, it's easier. But by easier I mean harder. Often our footer stories are ones that we choose not to think about and keep tucked deep within us. They can be painful or make us feel guilt or shame. Maybe we've only ever told our best friend, or no one at all. But in doing the work to explore these stories, how they made you feel, and the impact that had on your life, you will discover the impact why for moving toward living a brave life.

There are three types of footer stories: the ones that make your heart explode, the stories that feel too painful to think about, and the third type are the stories that haven't happened or been told yet—your wildest dreams or your deepest desires that you don't dare tell a soul.

Your footer stories are what help you discover your impact why. When we understand our impact why, we can tap into our super (why) power, launching us into living a brave life. A life with purpose. A life where even when we're afraid, we act anyway. A life where we're so connected to our own initiatives and mission that we're now able to say no to the wrong things and yes to the right things. Without hesitation or guilt. A life where we no longer overvalue stability. But instead, a life where we're in constant pursuit of fulfillment.

In the next chapter I'll share (very uncomfortably) some of my own footer stories. And believe me, it is hard. But I hope in doing so it will allow the space for grace in your own life and the ability to look into your own footer stories to discover your why.

So...

"I'm just gonna brave it..."

(Ish is about to get real, y'all.)

Reflect before you Neglect.

Write here:

What are some of the generalized whys you have for your life?

. . . .

. . . .

. . . .

. . . .

. . . .

Before digging into your footer stories, what do you "think" your why is?

. . . .

. . . .

. . . .

. . . .

. . . .

. . . .

put that

THING DOWN

FLIP IT

FLIP IT

and REVERSE

IT

CHAPTER FIVE:

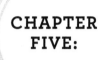
Footer Stories

Once upon a time, not too long ago, I was....

Not a ho.

If you knew me in my late teens/early twenties you may be shocked to read this. But it's true. I was not a ho. As I shared in my foundation stories, I was very involved in church through-out my teens. Most of my closest friendships were with those I went to church with. When I moved from Alabama to Virginia in the beginning of my 10th-grade year, I dated a guy from my youth group for around a year. I wouldn't let the guy get past first base. I'm actually not sure he ever really stepped foot on first base if I'm being completely honest.

I wore my virginity ring (gold band with emeralds and diamonds) on my wedding ring finger like it was a badge of honor and the weight of what the ring meant wasn't lost on me. I once lost my ring (not my virginity) in my room, and I cried for an hour, only to find that it had fallen off my dresser into the laundry pile. Imagine how I was going to feel when I actually lost my virginity!

Now, I was not perfect and much had changed by my senior year. But the values of virtue that had been instilled in me growing up still held true. I had a second long-term boyfriend, who also shared my faith, but as time went on, one thing led to another and—spoiler alert—I had to take the ring off. A few months later my young heart was broken by a breakup. That's when everything started to change.

The guy I had been dating had become part of the popular crowd. As soon as he broke up with me, he began to date another girl, who was also a part of the popular crowd. Being that I was the last long-term girlfriend, I guess I became enemy #1 by default. These girls, some of whom I'd considered to be friends at earlier points in time, were relentless.

The whispers, talking behind my back, bursts of laughter as I walked past them in the hall, calling me names in the parking lot, actually throwing a water bottle at me while everyone looked on and laughed and writing, "Amy Paitsel is a ho," on the back of a bathroom stall door were just a few of their tactics. I was a wuss and didn't stand up for myself. I thought if I just lay low, then over time it would stop. But I think it made things worse because I was an easy target.

The saddest part to me is when I look back, even through all of those things, I would still hope to be accepted by those girls. When they would talk to me individually when no one else was around I truly thought they were trying to be my friends. I let them use me for rides at times to places, realizing once there they were embarrassed to be seen with me and would continue to talk about me behind my back. I felt a desire to seek acceptance and hoped that if I remained kind, I would feel worthy enough to be accepted. Only to feel over and over that I was less than.

It was during this time that I dropped out of school. But removing myself from that environment didn't stop the talking and rumors. These things spilled from high school into life after. Rumors became a reality. The things that were being said became truths and this created issues in relationships.

I remember the guy I dated after high school saying to me once that he was dating me despite what people said or thought of me. Like I should be thanking him or giving him credit for dating someone "like me." After we broke up, what I found was although I was hopeful when a new guy would show interest in me, it wasn't always for the right reasons. For those who took the time to get to know me and I really thought liked me, even if they did, there was always a sense of embarrassment around dating me.

I guess I was naive but every single guy I dated, "talked to," spent time with, or "hung out with," I truly thought liked me and wanted to date me. But they didn't, or at least wouldn't admit they did because, well, I had a bad reputation.

Most of what was said about me wasn't true. Probably 80%. Once the rumors started, it seemed as if everyone was jumping on the bandwagon. The number of notches in belts people claimed I was vs. what I actually was may have been 3 to 1. Have you ever heard a rumor so good about yourself you couldn't even believe it? I was always astonished by the things I heard, like... "Oh my gracious, and what did I do next?" or better yet "who?"

I was fortunate to have real friends who knew me and knew the truth. I wish I would have focused more on that. I spent a lot of time between 18 and 20 feeling embarrassed about who I was, and feeling less than others for actions I never even did. But over time if you continuously hear things about yourself, you begin to believe that at least part must be true. Maybe people see things about you that you don't see yourself. Maybe you really are an embarrassment. Maybe you really aren't worthy of love and acceptance. Maybe you are less than.

Let's flip a coin

I always imagine the thrill that group of girls must have felt when they heard that at 20, I was pregnant. Like it was confirmation of all the rumors and things they'd always said about me. I was ashamed. I had only been dating my son's father for around three months when this happened. Although I was working full time, I was still living at home with my parents. Unwed. I had little clue what I wanted to do with my life to provide for myself, much less to provide for another.

In some ways it was confirmation for me too of the things that were said about me. When I took the pregnancy test alone in the bathroom and I saw the two lines, I was so disappointed in myself. I cried harder than I ever remembered crying before. I remember feeling a weight of let down—for my parents, my friends, my church, those who stood by me regardless of what others said about me. But the deepest let down was that of myself. In that moment I felt that any chance I had for redemption was gone.

Regardless of my shame, I knew I needed to suck it up, buttercup, and brave it anyway. I had to go and tell a man I had only really known for four months or so that I was pregnant with his child. I felt sick, and not from morning sickness.

I'm not sure that there is a right way to have this conversation. But for me, for whatever reason, having it in the Capital One cafeteria seemed to make the most sense. To say he was shocked was an understatement, but what he did next still shocks me to this day.

Once what I had just said registered with him, he reached into his pocket and pulled out a coin and said, "Heads we keep it, tails we don't." I'm not even kidding, ladies, his solution to this "problem" was a flip of a coin. To which I said, "You can flip that coin as many times as you like. You can be involved or not, but I'm keeping this baby."

It wasn't planned. I knew it was going to be hard, it deepened my shame and lack of self-worth, but I knew this baby's life was a gift from God, and termination, <u>for me</u>, was never a consideration. (I underlined "for me" because I feel that this is truly a personal decision. What is right for me is/was that regardless of the circumstances, a life given to me was never up for consideration. At the same time, I would never speak of or judge another for a decision they make for themselves. We need to remember sometimes that God is the only true judge and he has called us to love, regardless of our differences, just love.)

The months that followed had their ups and downs. My son's father had a hard time accepting things, and I really don't blame him; it was hard. He was embarrassed and became more and more distant, blaming me for the pregnancy and ruining his life. We barely knew each other but felt pressure to get married from our families, which in the beginning felt like a good idea. Until the day I remember standing in the back hall at Capital One and he told me, "I don't want to marry you," to which I replied, "Good, I don't want to marry you either." But on the inside, it felt like more confirmation that I was not worthy of love or redemption.

About five months in, I had a doctor's appointment on a Friday and my son's father never showed, which wasn't completely strange. But after the appointment, there were no calls, no anything. Until that Tuesday when he called nonchalantly and told me he had gone for the weekend to a 311 concert with friends. (I learned later it was "a" friend, whom I heard he was dating a week after this phone call). I was taken aback but in true Amy form I didn't even act mad or ask why he would do that and not say anything to me or let me know he was leaving. Besides, if I knew anything about myself to this point it was that I should be grateful for what I got as it related to relationships with men. I hung up and then finally something came over me. I called him back and when he answered I said, "I wouldn't be with you if I wasn't pregnant and you were treating me this way, so I'm not going to stay with you just because I am." (See the glimmer of bravery? Maybe there was a chance for redemption in me.)

I braved the last four months of the pregnancy on my own, with the support of my family, of course. My sweet dad even offered to go to Lamaze classes with me. (I bought him a shirt to wear to class that said "Grandpa" because I didn't want people getting it twisted).

On June 13, 2000, my life changed. I gave birth to a perfect baby boy, Michael Brayden Scott Paitsel. Nothing else in the world mattered. I may have felt that I wasn't worthy of love, but I was going to pour every ounce of love I had into this little boy, and I was sure as heck going to work every day to be worthy of being his momma.

Two Baby Daddies

Dating as a single mom proved difficult. We've already established my lack of self-worth and now add on the additional baggage of being a single mother. We were a package deal. It already seemed difficult enough to ask for someone to love and accept me (because of my mindset, not because it was true). Now I needed to also ask someone to love and accept my son as well. Bonus was that his biological father had joined the Army and had very little involvement other than the occasional check-in. This seemed good in that it didn't create drama for anyone else, but it was bad in that he didn't help support Brayden. I was solely supporting myself and my son, which meant anyone who married me would have to step up and do the same.

That's when I met my ex-husband. Do you know how they say that history often repeats itself? Well, about a year into our rocky relationship I found out I was pregnant. Yep, if there was ever a question about my fertility, that was put to rest. I'm fairly certain I could think myself pregnant if I wanted to.

When I do things, I tend to go all in, so if I was going to live a life of shame, I was going to make sure to double up on that and be the best at it. So, there I was again, 22, still unwed, single mother, preggo with my second child.

This time, regardless of the circumstances, I was not going to be a single mother with two baby daddies. So at 22, at five months pregnant, in my parents' living room, I got married.

By 23, I was married with a seven-year-old stepdaughter, a three-year-old son, a newborn and the self-worth of a stink bug. Meanwhile, my friends were finishing college, launching careers, going out on the weekends, traveling, and figuring out life.

I was young, and so was he. We were both far from perfect. He is a great father to our youngest son. We have both evolved and are different people today than we were then. This footer story, in particular, has many, many more layers. As I mentioned before, your footer stories are ones you don't like to share and may never tell a soul. So, I ask for grace as it relates to this one in ending it here.

Your Hamster Died

If you're a parent and you've ever had to utter those words (you can replace hamster with fish, cat, dog, or turtle), you know how difficult and heartbreaking it can be. It's never easy to be the one to share something with your child that you know will break their heart. There's no way you can protect them from the pain they feel, although in this case I would have given anything for it to have been a hamster.

As I mentioned earlier, my first son's father was in and out of his life from the time I found out I was pregnant. I'm not one who holds a grudge. You've probably figured out by now that my toxic trait is that I always hope for the best in others regardless of past experiences. So, at times he would show up again and I would never deny him, or Brayden, the opportunity to connect.

Because he was in the Army, he was gone most of Brayden's childhood. He served all over, even spending time in Iraq during the war. He was a front-line medic and saw heartbreaking, mind-altering things that made it very difficult to cope, especially given his own upbringing.

I didn't know until after finding out I was pregnant that the parents he had introduce me to as his own were actually his foster parents. He had been abused as a young child and was removed from that home and placed into the hands of the state. The empathy I have for anyone, especially a child who can't help themselves, is unmeasurable. And to understand the impact of that trauma on someone is not something I can pretend to begin to do.

During his service, he was blown off a ladder and suffered a brain injury that at the time seemed mild but allowed him an honorable discharge. His injury classified him as disabled, and he was sent home. At this time Brayden was about six years old.

Once home, he struggled to transition back to civilian life. He had suffered from depression and anxiety prior to enlisting. His time of service and the things he experienced only amplified those issues. He had difficulties overcoming a sense of despair, but his one shining light that kept him going and wanting to get better was Brayden. He would show up at times and then disappear again for months at a time, even as much as a year.

During that time, he was in and out of VA homes and hospitals. He began suffering from seizures and severe PTSD and was eventually classified as clinically insane by the state of Virginia and 100% disabled, complete and total.

Brayden's father may have been absent but what was not was his love for his son. To see the way he looked at Brayden and marveled at the fact that he had something to do with his being was to experience seeing what true love looked like. And Brayden marveled at his father. He so desired his time, love, and affection. He saw the relationship between my youngest son and his father and so desperately wanted to feel that same sense of love and acceptance from a father in the biological sense.

As Brayden's father struggled, he would distance himself for long periods of time. Now looking back, I see that it wasn't out of selfishness but in trying to do what was best for Brayden. His hope was to work toward a better version of himself for Brayden.

It was during a time of distance where we hadn't heard from his father in several months when I received a phone call from his father's foster mom asking me to call her. My heart instantly sank. I knew something must be wrong for her to call.

On Monday, May 5, 2014, my son's father passed away from an accidental overdose. Brayden was 13 years old at the time. As much of a roller coaster those 13 years had been, my heart broke.

It broke for his father who had lost his life and the chance to restore his life and his relationship with his son. And it broke knowing that the hope of my son to someday have a normal relationship with his dad was now never going to be a reality. And it broke knowing that I was going to have to be the one to break my son's heart telling him his father was gone.

I'll never forget that day. The green of the paint of my son's room at the time, his face as he wondered why I came in with such a serious demeanor with something to tell him, or the look on his face when I told him his father was gone. I, myself, fought back tears as my son's heart was shattered. The feeling I felt that he had just lost something that I could never replace, or fill, no matter how much I loved or showed up. Again, for me it was a reminder of being less than.

We do the best we can in all situations as parents. Sometimes that's all we can give regardless of how not the best our best is.

I love Jesus AND I love the Gays

Have I mentioned that I grew up in church? A couple of times, right? I've been Methodist, Baptist, Assembly of God, Non-denominational, and I'm sure there's a few I'm forgetting. I remember the fear I had of sin. Praying in my head quickly as a little girl after telling a white lie in case I was struck down by lightning right after. Wanted to always make sure I had my ticket into heaven. Faith of a mustard seed? That's me. I never questioned or researched, just knew what I had been taught my whole life to be true.

Now, we all know I wasn't perfect. I mean those girls from high school would have called me more "ho-ly" than Holy. But I did try to live a life based on the values and morals I had been taught no matter how often I failed. And I was/am well versed in the Bible and what it says is right and wrong. (My mom used to pay me for memorizing Bible verses. John 11:35 was my favorite and gave the biggest return on investment.)

If you're familiar with the Bible, you've probably heard of the King James version, the English Standard version, the Living Testament version, the New International Version. Well with experience and exposure in life, you start to form your own understanding and version as it relates to life. And if you have a close relationship with God, I think he intends it that way.

Because my heart had always had a desire for grace, empathy, love, and acceptance, my tendency was to give that to others. So, although I was rooted in faith, and I know what the Bible says is right and wrong, I always kept an open mind as it related to others.

That's easy to say when you aren't the one on the hot seat. I believed in waiting till marriage, until I didn't. We've all had good intentions as it relates to avoiding sin, until we sin. We've all sinned and fallen short. It's easier to love others through their sin than it is to deal with sin in our own lives. At least for me. I can't say that's the case for all Christians.

I've seen some pretty brutal handlings of sin from churches that make me wonder how a whole congregation full of people who've never sinned can come together to call out another's sin and condemn them. I didn't realize God had delegated that role and created whole congregations of people who themselves have never sinned so are worthy of judging in this manner. (Insert eye roll here.)

Anyway, when my oldest son was 14, I learned he was gay. Or wait, wait, correction, he **told** me he was gay. I knew he was gay at about two years old, or had my suspicions, I guess. But he officially came out to me when he was in eighth grade.

Prior to having my son, I don't know that I had an opinion on nurture vs. nature. But what I did have an opinion on was that I knew that God didn't make mistakes. And secondly, I had raised my son and knew him better than anyone. He was who he is since the day he was born. SO you can imagine my parent heart loved him beyond measure, but my Christian "teachings" mind was pretty confused.

I've had people ask me how I feel or handle having gay children as a believer. (My oldest stepdaughter too has since come out to me.) The truth is how I **feel** is that I couldn't be more proud of my children. I love who God created them to be and I love that he gave them to me to raise. He truly doesn't make mistakes.

Shortly after Brayden told me he was gay, I was driving down Harrowgate Road in Chester, VA, listening to the song "Same Love" by Macklemore. As I came to the stoplight to turn onto route 10, the words, "And I can't change, even if I tried, even if I wanted to," played. In that moment I spoke out loud in prayer and said, "What am I supposed to do, God? What am I supposed to do? I know your word, but I also know my son. So, what am I supposed to do?"

Before the light could turn green and I could formulate another thought, I heard five words that were not of my own, that would forever change my life.

"You're supposed to love him."

Wow! "You're supposed to love him." No more beautiful words to that point in my life had ever been spoken. And in that moment, I realized that THAT was what I had been called to do. I had been given this child to love him. Not to judge or condemn or to play God with, but to LOVE.

From that day forward I chose that in all things I was going to choose love as it related to my son, and to others. To things I don't understand, or I can't relate to. That we ALL (myself included) are worthy of love, God's love and the love of others.

So, I choose love. Forever, love.

Skin and Bones and Hidden Spending

We've all heard the term "financial freedom." Well, the true definition of this is "a state in which an individual or household has accumulated sufficient financial resources to cover its living expenses without having to depend on work to maintain its current lifestyle." However, to me, it meant something very different in my 20s.

Financial freedom to me was wanting the ability to walk into the store, see something I liked, and buy it. Without asking, without permission, without being told ahead of time I could or being given an allowance for shopping once a year.

Money was tight for me in more ways than one. Tight because we were a family of five with a limited income. But also, tight because I had no say or control when it came to the finances. I had grown up in a traditional household where my dad was the provider and my mother stayed home. As I mentioned earlier, we too struggled at times financially. So, living on a budget wasn't out of the scope of reality for me. But although I was also contributing, I thought that the right thing to do was to hand over my paycheck every two weeks and never make any suggestion or request on how money should be spent.

I was given an allowance of $100 every two weeks for spending money (so $50 a week) to spend on incidentals—food when I forgot to pack extras for myself or the kids, sometimes gas. I gave up complete control as it related to any decision-making because I thought that was the role of the wife.

I thought I was doing the right thing and being a good wife, but over time the control I gave up started to feel like control placed on me. I felt like I was suffocating. The problem is that when we give up too much control over ourselves and our decisions, we spiral, desperately grasping for any sense of control or sense of "being." My dad used to always say that the problem in a relationship where one person acts as the parent (has all the say) and one as the child (has no say) is that eventually the child grows up and wants to move out.

This created issues for me as a need to seek out happiness in things that gave me a feeling of control. You begin to justify behaviors that bring you a sense of control. And in some weird way, those things bring you a sense of "adulting" and happiness. Even if they're ultimately destructive.

For me, one of the things I felt I could control was my weight. I had always been smaller-figured but needed to control what

I ate, and my workout habits became an obsessive thing. It's hard to differentiate something that society says is good for you—eating healthy and working out—and something that's harmful because of the source of the motivation. At my most extreme, I limited myself to 800 calories a day and under 20 grams of fat. I worked out daily and felt an immense amount of happiness and satisfaction with the scale number as it dropped. At my lowest, I was 106 pounds at 28 years old. (I'm 5'6" with an athletic build, so this was extreme). My mother-in-law said I looked like a skeleton; I remember feeling a sense of pride about that statement, like it was a compliment.

After having a conversation with a friend about her past eating disorder, I decided to put weight on. Part of the control was also being able to decide that it was too much and that it wasn't controlling me but that I controlled it. So, putting weight back on meant I was still in control. This was really the point in my life where negative self-talk began. I still struggle at times with this. Someone said I looked "healthy" as a compliment after I had gained five pounds and I cried. As much as I could control my weight, both up and down, I still couldn't control what other people thought, nor could I control the issues I had with self-worth as it related to my weight. I struggled for years with feeling too skinny or too big, never just right. I envied other women who had the ability to love their bodies, as it wasn't something I was able to do.

During this time, I had started working at my first builder. I went from working at a call center where jeans and t-shirts were appropriate to an office where most all the women had designer purses and shoes. When I started, I had two work-appropriate outfits to my name. A jean wrap dress from Victoria's Secret (that I not only wore for my interview but also on my first day) and a shirt and skirt from Target. I had one pair of brown open-toe wedges that luckily matched both outfits. I packed my lunch every day the first two weeks so I could purchase a pair of black pants and two sweaters with my spending money that week at Target. I also borrowed a pair of my mom's black shoes to match, even though they were a half size too big. Talk about feeling like an imposter! Luckily Fridays were causal, so I was set there. But I had to get really creative in styling the few things I had so they would look different each day. I remember one week I wore the black pants three of the five days, praying every day that I wouldn't spill anything on them.

Week three I borrowed pieces from a good friend who worked at the J.Crew call center. (She got an employee discount.) I remember how good I felt wearing those items. In those moments I felt like I fit in with the sales girls. It made me feel like I belonged and was not "less than" for once. A false sense of being worthy. I remember one day one of the girls said she loved my skirt and asked where I got it. It felt so good to say "J.Crew."

Our office building was across the street from a new outdoor mall and many of the girls I worked with would go over on their lunch break to eat and shop. This created a dilemma for me because I couldn't afford to do both. If I wanted to have lunch with them each day, I needed to make sure I had money to pay for food and couldn't shop, but if I shopped, I wouldn't be able to have money for lunch and it would be odd for me to go over and sit while they ate.

It was a couple months in and I had stopped by my mom's on my way home because she said there was mail there for me. When I opened the mail it was a credit card that I'd had prior to getting married that was paid off. I guess I never closed the account and the old card that I'd gotten rid of expired, so they sent a new one. But not just that, they had upped my credit limit to $2,500.

Two Thousand Five Hundred Dollars!!!! Like whaaaaaa.......

I had never had a limit that high. I felt a sense of pride because it made me feel like such an adult. I had never had money like that before at one time. I put the card in my (Target) purse, not thinking much more about it. That is, until a week later when we went over for lunch and stopped in ALDO after. I was doing my casual "just looking" walk while the other girls shopped, when I came across a pair of classic nude patent leather round-toe pumps. Nude? That basically goes with everything and the shoe is basically a classic; anyone who invests in the shoe will be wearing them for a lifetime. I flipped them over and to my surprise they were on sale for $38 (originally priced at $79). They were basically free. (If you save more than you spend, that basically means they're free.) I didn't have the $38, BUT it was only $38. I could buy them on the card and then pay for them when I got my next allowance and no one would be the wiser. I was just giving myself an advance. The bill still went to my mom's house so I was good there and I could deposit my cash into my old checking account and write the check from there.

I walked toward the register shoes in hand, the last size 6.5 at that, when one of the girls I was with said, "You're getting those?? Oh my gosh, I love them, they're classic." To which I replied with pride, "I know, right?" With one swipe of the card, the shoes were mine and I had started down what would become a very slippery slope for myself.

The shoes became a shirt, which became a dress, which became a purse. The $38 charge became $100, which became $200, which became $500. My $200 a month allowance became cash advances, which became balance transfers. Before I knew it, I had racked up debt that I had no way of paying off. I compartmentalized the fear of the debt and justified that I should be able to own these things, like the other girls, because I was an adult and I worked just as hard. And the happiness and false sense of worth I felt in wearing the items outweighed the fear of the debt tenfold.

I hid the debt for years. The longer I hid it, the greater it became. I was searching for happiness and freedom in something that was making me upset and imprisoned.

I ended up going to my parents for help and my parents paid off my debt for me. My father worked a year past retirement to help. That was unconditional love and acceptance but the guilt I felt from creating that situation I still carry today.

I'm not sure how my ex-husband didn't notice as my closet grew from a few things to a full closet. He didn't learn about the debt until just before our divorce.

These control issues haunt me to this day. Both are not things that are easy to talk about, but I know that I'm not the only one struggling from these types of secrets. I recognize that this journey isn't just mine—so I tell it for others facing similar struggles. I'd love to say through some miraculous event I was cured of these issues, but I still struggle with freedom, self-love, and spending. It takes coming to terms with the bad habits we have and understanding the roots of the issues to reshape our relationships with these things.

Embracing healthier habits and self-love becomes your compass. Just know you're not alone. Mistakes in life don't make you less than or not worthy of having the life you want to create for yourself. We can all start over and make better decisions focused on living a life that's more fulfilled so we aren't seeking it in what brings us struggles.

He's my Hero

Lamaze classes and paid debt, Roy McCutchen Paitsel was a one-of-a-kind kinda man. My father was my hero from the day I was born. He worked hard to provide, and he never gave up. He left his stresses at work so he could show up at home as the best father possible. He went without so we could have, never letting my siblings and me see how much he and my mother struggled. He taught me imagination, work ethic, humor, and love.

One of the greatest things about me is that I came from him. I'm eternally grateful he was chosen to be my father.

2015 proved to be one of my hardest years to date. I had recently been promoted to sales manager. This new role was daunting, especially being that I had never been in sales. The stress to perform and be successful as a sales leader was heavy. I was relentless in my pursuit to prove I was worthy of the role.

In July, I lost my grandfather, who was the second greatest man I've ever met. They lived in Michigan, and I didn't see them as much as I would have liked growing up. It was even less as an adult. But the profound impact that man had on all who knew him was evident. He was a stern man, with the sweetest soul, and loved beyond measure.

Early that summer my dad had to undergo surgery on his legs to open the vein grafts that were beginning to close. What was supposed to be a pretty routine surgery turned into two months in the hospital due to infection and setbacks in his recovery.

Prior to this, my mother had planned to take a three-week trip to Utah with my youngest son to visit my sister in August. As the timing for the trip approached, it seemed more and more unlikely that she could go. My father was slated to go home the day before my mother's trip. What was evident to me was that my mother needed this trip and the time away, but my father also was ready to come home but would need additional care.

I was asked to take care of my father during this time, to which of course I agreed. For 21 days, I would go over to my parents' house around 6 a.m. to give him his medicine and hook him up to a portable IV that would administer an antibiotic. I made sure he had breakfast and anything else he needed for the day. Then I'd drive an hour to work, work a full day, drive back an hour to my parents' to hook my dad back up to the IV. Made sure he had dinner, sometimes stopping to buy groceries on my way back down. Did the dishes and any cleaning necessary. Made sure my dad's incision was healing and staying clean. Took him to any doctor's appointments needed. And each evening drove home to do dinner, dishes, homework, and bedtime for my family.

In these seasons in life when we're grinding day after day after day, it's easy to get burned out. I think it was sometime during week two that I had my breakdown moment, calling my sister in tears because the demands at work, the guilt I was feeling being away from my family from 5:30 a.m. until after 7:30 p.m., and the stress of taking care of my dad but not wanting him to feel he was a burden, all felt like too much. But what I love about the female spirit is that we can have these breakdown moments—sometimes that's all we really need—and shake it off, put on our big girl panties, and get back to grinding. And that's what I did. I decided to be present, where my feet were, during that time, letting the next moment take care of itself.

As adults, it's rare that we get to spend that much time with our parents. The situation wasn't going to change so I had to change my mindset and appreciate the time with my dad. Instead of scrolling on my phone and answering emails while the ball of antibiotics worked itself through the IV, I started having conversations with my dad. My favorite was sitting on the front porch with him reading to him from the Bible since he wasn't able to leave the house to attend church. I snapped a photo one Sunday because I knew it was a moment I wouldn't want to forget. I'm so glad I did; it's one of my favorite photos I have.

You can see the IV bag hanging from around his neck and how frail he'd become from his time in the hospital. But what I love is the peace on his face as he listened to me read to him from Proverbs. The other thing I love about this photo is that my dad is wearing plaid boxer shorts, which he'd only discovered for the first time during his time of recovery. (He was more of a tighty-whities man.) The first time I came over and he was wearing them, he said to me, "Amy, would you believe these are underwear? After I get better I can wear these to the grocery store. Ha, ha." To which I replied, "Sure, Dad, if you want."

They say it takes 21 days to make a habit. I spent 21 days with my dad during that summer of 2015. Looking back, no matter how difficult some of the days felt, spending time with him was the best habit I ever made. He went from my father to my best friend during this time. We had always been close, but our bond was stronger than ever.

Once my mom returned, life went back to as normal as it could. Between work and kids and regular daily routines.

In September, I asked my husband for a divorce after years of being unhappy and not vocalizing it to him. My biggest regret in our relationship was not speaking up and telling him how I felt. Often when we're unhappy in a situation or relationship, we don't acknowledge our contribution to our own unhappiness and only focus on the other person. I take full credit for my part in the failure of our marriage. It was hard, and I was scared—but I braved it.

During this time the grafts in my dad's legs had shut back down. He had to go back into surgery for a second time to have them reopened. I struggled with hearing this because in my opinion if I go to a hairdresser and they give me a bad haircut I typically don't go back to that same hairdresser to let them have another go at it. But the decision wasn't mine to make.

His second surgery was originally scheduled for Tuesday, December 1. The doctor had an emergency and had to delay to Friday, the 4th. Thursday the 3rd, my youngest son had an orchestra concert that my dad was able to attend because of this delay. When they say you never know the last moments you'll have with someone, they're right. I still vividly remember standing outside the auditorium beside my dad as he hugged my son and told him he was proud of him.

I had planned on going with my mom and dad to the hospital on the day of surgery. When the date changed, I had a previous commitment to go to, a gymnastics meet in Virginia Beach, so instead I went to my mom and dad's house before leaving. There was something about that morning that felt different to me. I'm not sure why, as my dad had multiple surgeries and procedures leading up to that day, but this one felt different.

I believe that God has a way of speaking to our hearts through intuition. I sat on the couch beside my dad's recliner and just stared at him. I felt the need to memorize him in that moment. I spent about 20 minutes with him before needing to say goodbye.

As I left, we hugged the longest hug we'd ever hugged. I told him I loved him and that, "If anything happens, you know I'll come back and take care of you, right?!" He nodded and told me he loved me too. I saw tears in his eyes; I could tell it felt different for him too.

When I got in the car, the tears began to flow and I couldn't explain why. It was the strangest feeling.

I waited throughout the day for updates from my mom but the anticipation was creating an anxiety that made me feel sick. The surgery took longer than expected. But finally in the late afternoon I received a text from my mom saying my dad was out of surgery and that all had gone well. I could finally breathe but I couldn't shake away the pit that I felt in my stomach.

After the gymnastics meet, we drove down to the beachfront to get dinner. As we were turning into the parking lot, an overwhelming feeling of sickness came over me. I felt a burning in my head and felt as if I was going to be sick. The feeling passed within a few minutes so we went into the restaurant. I hoped that a glass of wine would take the edge off. We were seated when my phone rang. It was my mom and she said, "Your dad came out of surgery and was in recovery and they believe he had a stroke. The doctor says I should call family and tell them to come now."

We drove back from Virginia Beach, a two-hour drive that felt like an eternity. I walked into the room and saw my dad, my best friend, lying in a coma state. I walked to him and leaned close to his ear and said, "I'm here, Dad. I told you I'd come back and take care of you." But my heart was crushed because I knew that there was nothing I could do. I spent the night, lying beside him, holding his hand, and asking him to hold on long enough for my sister to make it there to say goodbye. She had jumped on a red-eye from Utah that night.

The next morning I called both my boys so I could place the phone to my dad's ear for them to tell him they loved him. Shortly after that, my sister arrived. My family stood around him holding hands, telling him we would take care of each other, and saying goodbye. Moments later the nurse walked in and checked his vitals and told us he was gone.

My dad always believed in me. He saw my value and my worth when I couldn't. From being there for every heartbreak, to loving me when life didn't go as planned, to bailing me out when I had nowhere to turn, he always knew I was worthy. Worthy of grace, worthy of investment, worthy of forgiveness, and worthy of love. The greatest gift we can give someone is the feeling of self-worth. My dad gave that tenfold; I just wish I would have believed it sooner.

When we lose someone who loves and believes in us, the greatest legacy we can carry in their honor is believing that the things they saw in us and knew to be true actually are. My dad was wise and thoughtful, and I respected him beyond measure. I looked for validation in the wrong things my whole life, when the only validation I truly needed was from those who knew me best. My dad was gone but he believed that I was not only capable, but worthy of doing anything I wanted to do. I decided it was time to start believing those things for myself. To love myself the way my dad loved me, flaws and all.

Sharing is Caring

And sometimes not sharing is caring too. These are just a few of my footer stories. To be honest, I didn't expect that writing this chapter would invoke as much emotion in me as it did. (I'm not a crier and I cried three times.) There are many more stories that I chose not to share because in not sharing I was practicing self-care for myself. You don't have to choose to share your footer stories with others; you may share some or none at all. And that's OK, but in doing the work to understand your footer stories, you'll learn more about your purpose. When I had to write these stories, it brought back all of the emotion and feelings I felt through each of those phases in life. I also explored the stories I chose not to share, stories of loss, hurt, guilt, and disappointment. But also, each story equally involves resilience, lessons, and bravery.

But what I recognized in exploring was a common theme throughout that clearly defined my impact why. Maybe you noticed it too. I hope that in doing the same you also find your purpose and why.

Reflect before you Neglect.

Write here:

Thinking about your footer stories, what common theme can you see?

. . . .

. . . .

. . . .

. . . .

How do these stories help you to understand your purpose and "Impact why"?

. . . .

. . . .

. . . .

. . . .

(_____) + (_____) + (_____) = Fulfillment

(Who) + (why) + (_____) = Fulfillment

You are
WORTHY

I am
WORTHY

CHAPTER SIX:

Expelled Bodily Products

Fooled ya! Nope, this is not a chapter about vomit or poop. The real title of this chapter is "My Why" but I didn't want you to cheat and skip chapters after I said that I was going to make you wait to hear my why. (I know how sneaky y'all can be.) So, I googled what the grossest things to read about were and "expelled bodily products" was one at the top on the list so I went with it to keep you from using the table of contents to skip ahead.

Worthy (/wer-<u>TH</u>e/) *adjective*:

- having or showing the qualities or abilities that merit recognition in a specified way
- deserving effort, attention, or respect
- good enough. suitable

My impact why. I am worthy. YOU are worthy.

If you were to ask me what the biggest difference between who I was a few years ago—not brave, no boundaries, no purpose, no fulfillment—and who I am today, it wasn't an issue of not being capable. (I was.) It wasn't that I didn't know I was capable. (I knew.) Believe me, I was born with the capable gene. I knew I was *capable* of doing anything I wanted to do. So, if that was a known truth, then what was the lie that was paralyzing me? (Insert meme of Wayne and Garth here: "We're not worthy!!") It was a question of worthiness. I didn't feel worthy. And I let experiences, words, situations, and life validate my fear of not being worthy. Of not being enough. I searched for fulfillment in the wrong things. I let guilt lead my decisions in life—as a daughter, a mother, a wife, an employee, and as a friend. But when I did that, I ended up failing those around me, and even more significant, I was failing myself. When this occurs, it becomes a cycle. I think I'm not worthy and I'm failing in life; I truly must not be worthy.

It took years for me to truly find a place of worthiness. Now, I'm not saying that every day is perfect. I still struggle some days with the negative talk. But I've found a place where I can be unbothered by it. We are **ALL** worthy of investment, success, trust, and love. That is my why power. That even in the moments of self-doubt, I can still push forward because I choose to be brave and I believe, like really believe, that I **am** worthy.

But more important to me is creating a space where other women feel the same way. The impact I want to make is to help other women reach their full potential by instilling in them a true sense of worthiness. So that we all get to a place of understanding that we're not just capable of doing anything we want but we're WORTHY of doing those things as well. Helping another individual to see their self-worth is one of the greatest gifts you can give. Almost all of us suffer from a lack of it. We need to help each other see our full potential, be each other's greatest cheerleaders, and remind one another of how talented, smart, trusted, loved, and worthy we all are.

A study done by SheSpeaks founder, Aliza Freud, found a large percentage of women (85%) say that they've struggled with low self-worth. The fact that almost an identical percentage (84%) report that their self-worth has a strong effect on their happiness also shows how feeling worthy is key in living a ful-filled life. It also means that there's a good chance that if you're reading this book, you, at some point, too, have had struggles with low self-worth. Or more than likely, you know of someone who has.

Let's face it; we live in a world where comparison is spoon-fed to us daily through almost every aspect of our lives. Social media is the straight-up CEO of comparison. And it's no mystery that the number one contributor of low self-worth is "comparing ourselves to others." That's followed closely by childhood expe-rience, negative self-talk (hello me), and relationship problems.

Apply the Missy Elliot technique (put it down, flip it, and reverse it) and what's on the other side of that? What things do women say contribute to a positive impact on self-worth? Family upbringing weighs in at 81%. (Find a family without dysfunc-tion and I'll find you a flying pig.) Then tying for second place are professional success and romantic relationships.

Ugggggggggghhhh-ga! Why are we relying on our families, our titles, and our romantic relationships (I just threw up a little in my mouth) to validate our self-worth, ladies?!?! No wonder so many of us struggle with this. We're looking to outside sources (imperfect sources at that) and asking them to validate our need for worth. What the even what?!? Hey, I'm not judging. I'm in the weeds of this with you. I allowed comparisons, family dynamics, past relationships, negative self-talk, and the need to achieve impact my self-worth. I checked all the dang boxes. All. Of. Them. (I clapped my hands on each of the periods.)

I had to learn to take those things back. The toxic relationships needed boundaries or to be let go of all together. I had to stop saying yes to everything and start saying yes to the right things. Stop looking to others (who really did not have any bearing on my worth or future) for validation. I needed to become unbothered by comparison and realize that the best version of me is the quirky, imperfect, goofy, raw version. That no title will ever validate my worth because the woman I was on the Sunday before the promotion I got on Monday was the same woman I woke up as on Tuesday.

I'll say it again...

I am worthy. YOU are worthy.

So, ask yourself right now...what are you capable of? And keep it real, y'all. Don't lie to yourself and say you believe you're capable of being the next GOAT, now that Serena retired, when you've never picked up a racket. (I'm speaking from experience; I actually did think this, and after $500 spent on equipment, buying cute outfit**s**...as in multiple...and spending two hours on the court, I realized I was probably wrong.)

(Not probably.)

But, but, but, there are two parts to this...

Also ask, what do I WANT to do? That's important—there are a lot of things I'm capable of but I don't want to do them. Y'all know I'm capable of cleaning some houses, and I'm mighty good at it too, but that doesn't mean I want to scrub your toilet the morning after Taco Tuesday! (Finally, some reference to our pretend chapter title—I knew I'd work it in somehow.)

If there's something you know you're capable of and you know you want to do, then ask yourself:

"Well, why the heck ain'tcha then?"

Because you CAN and more importantly YOU ARE WORTHY. I'm living proof. It's not conceit. It's that I know that:

(Who) + (Why) + (_____) = Fulfillment

(Oooooh, this is getting so exciting!)

If you did the work to understand your who (foundation), and then your why (footer), then you might be asking yourself *how* you take those truths and use them to live a life that will bring you fulfillment?

...Dang, how quickly you forgot...y'all know that *my why* is to help you see your full potential and that you're not just capable but also WORTHY of that life... so I got you...I mean, by now y'all already know what I'm going to say...

You just gotta brave it.

But how? I got you, girl...

(Don't you dare stop reading and put your bookmark on this page; it's the cliff-hanger chapter. Flip the dang page!)

Reflect before you Neglect.

Write here:

What is the life you're not only capable of achieving, but worthy of having?

....

....

....

....

....

....

How does *YOUR "Impact why"* create a purposeful fulfilled life for you?

....

....

....

....

....

BREATHE

embrace fear

and TRUST

YOURSELF

CHAPTER SEVEN:

The How

"How" is the last factor in the equation of living a fulfilling life.

$$(who) + (why) + (how) = Fulfillment$$

But here's the good news, I'm going to give this one to ya! No homework to understand your how. Just one word. Brave.

If being brave was a sport, I'd like to believe I could go pro, and not just pro but I'd be a first-round draft pick. I practice bravery on the daily and even call myself a brave expert. Just like with anything, the more you do it, the better you become. I sound pretty bad a$$ right now, right?!? Like, if there were a zombie apocalypse, you'd definitely want to track me down as your protector. (I love a good ole zombie apocalypse.)

But remember earlier when I said brave is a verb? It's an action. And also remember just a few sentences ago when I said that I practice bravery on the daily...well truth is, in order to practice bravery you have to be what?

Afraid.

Yep, that's right. No need to be brave if you aren't afraid, right?!? I'm just one big ole scaredy-cat. A phony! I'm an expert in being brave because I have to be. Because let's face it, life is scary. And I'm not talking about the Walking Dead herd of zombies chasing you kind of scary. (Yay, zombies!) I'm talking about the day-to-day pressures, expectations, tasks, mistakes, need to show up for ourselves and for others that we all place on ourselves every day.

Studies estimate that the average adult makes around 35,000 decisions daily. Now, what are the chances that one of those decisions could be a wrong one? Or how about the fact that 70% of us experience imposter syndrome at some point in our lives? What about when we overcommit and are overwhelmed and just don't have the capacity to see things through? Or how about when we fail as a parent, friend, or spouse? Ugh, for-getting to do something we were supposed to do. Or asked to do something outside our comfort zones? Or just turn on the news and the weight of the world in its current state rests on us. (I'd almost prefer a zombie apocalypse most days.) And the seasons of life when we're dealing with much more...death, divorce, sickness, depression...the list could go on and on.

(Jeez, just writing that paragraph gave me anxiety.)

Phew, being brave in today's world can seem exhausting. Impossible even. Forget the long-term aspirations and goals; it's hard to get past just the daily needs to show up and be brave. So even if we've done the work to first figure out *who* we are and then the *why* behind the impact we want to make, then *how* the heck do we find it in us to be brave enough to take the steps toward creating the life we want in order to be fulfilled? I have your mind spinning now, don't I?!? So where do we start? Seven simple words.

Breathe and put that ish down, girl.

Just put it down. Breathe for a second. I give you permission. No really, I'm telling you it's OK. And not just OK, but we NEED to do it at times. I think sometimes we need someone to give us permission to take it all off for a second. (Bow-chica-wow-wow.) (Sorry, I typed "take it all off" and my mind instantly went there.)

But seriously, no one is denying that life can be a lot some-times. So, it can seem impossible to work toward the things we want that align with our impact why that we haven't yet accomplished. But it's OK. We need to learn how to take it off, like, take it allllll off. (You did it this time, didn't you? Wink. Wink.) Take the crap off (not your clothes) and breathe. The first step to being brave is to first, just breathe. You see people pass out when they get scared? It's because they forget to breathe. So, let's start there. Just. Breathe.

Seems like a simple start, I know, but taking a second to breathe when you're about to do something brave can help you cope more mindfully as it relates to situations and can improve the way you think about the situation and about yourself. Breathing can also help you move past fear because it helps you to move past emotions like fear by focusing on your breath instead of fearful thoughts.

You breathing? Good. Now let's get to work.

Now that we've given ourselves permission to breathe and shed the weight of the fear, how do we then become brave to move toward a life of fulfillment? I wish it were as easy as just throwing caution to the wind and jumping in headfirst, but it'll take a whole lot more than breathing to get you past fear.

Dr. Kerry Ressler, director of the Neurobiology of Fear Laboratory at McLean Hospital, said, "Talking about being fearless covers up where people really are with fear. After all, fear is the most evolutionarily conserved behavioral reflex for survival." What that tells me is that to truly be fearless you would then lack the commonsense triggers for mere survival. (Those are the ones who die first during a zombie apocalypse). So, there's actually no such thing as being fearless really, only such a thing as being dumb.

That considered, I'm not so sure I want to be considered fearless. I'd honestly rather be known for being afraid. True story.

Think about it. Being afraid makes you pause and consider the implications of the action you're about to take. Sounds pretty responsible if you ask me. Ressler also said, "Fear produces the same responses in people now as it did in the beginning of human history. We've needed fear to survive as a species, to run from the lion crouching in the brush, and we still need it." We shouldn't be striving toward something as unattainable and reckless as fearlessness. We should embrace fear and be OK with being afraid, but brave. The real question is, how do you not let the emotional response of the fear reflex run wild and keep you paralyzed from moving forward or taking risk when it will pay off in a positive way?

Fear should keep you from jumping off a building but it shouldn't keep you from moving toward a life of fulfillment. The good news is that in the same way that fear protects us when something bad happens that scares us and keeps us from repeating the same action, it also produces dopamine in the brain which elicits pleasure when we overcome something positive that we were fearful of.

If you've ever had to speak in front of a large group, you probably know this feeling: the complete overwhelming fear you feel before stepping on stage and the dopamatic high you feel after you step off the stage. Both generate from the same place and action but the after high is the feeling that helps you to continue stepping outside your comfort zone to stretch yourself even further. You go from **having** to give a speech against your will, to not minding, to volunteering and looking for opportunities. Doesn't mean you're not afraid each time you step out on stage. It just means that you're still afraid, but brave. Over time, you become well practiced in bravery. And doing things that make you afraid become easier.

One of my favorite quotes of all time was by Neil Gaiman, author of "Coraline," when he wrote, "Being brave doesn't mean you aren't scared. Being brave means you are scared, really scared, badly scared, and you do the right thing anyway." When you're doing things that align with your impact why and move you toward a brave life of fulfillment, you're doing the right thing for you, even if you're scared.

Brave means doing things despite being scared. So why not normalize being afraid? Embrace it. We need to stop being afraid of, well, being afraid. We all are fearful at times. (Well, except for those dumb fearless folks getting their limbs chomped on by zombies.) So, burn the workout top that says "Fearless" on it and embrace your inner scaredy-cat. (I feel like we need a whole new line of women's workout clothing with the phrase "Afraid, but Brave.")

You can't brave something that you aren't fearful of, and if it doesn't scare you, is it really worth doing anyway?

Breathe. Embrace Fear. And...

You know *who* you are, right?!? And you know your *why* and the impact you want to make, correct?!? We've also established that you're not only capable but worthy. If you truly have figured these things out, then...Trust yourself.

One of our biggest issues as women is we don't allow ourselves to trust our own selves. (Ugh, this kills me!! How much time we got, 'cause, girl, I'm about to preach).

I want to discuss the origin of this first, THEN we'll talk about how we overcome our embraced fear and lack of trust to put brave into action.

When we're young, we're taught not to disappoint. Not to hurt other people's feelings regardless of our own discomfort.

"Give Uncle Barry a hug."

"Go to the banquet with my friend's son as a favor."

"Don't embarrass me."

"Don't embarrass yourself."

"Don't be rude or say no when someone offers you something even if you don't want it."

"Smile and nod."

"Be a good girl."

Are you cringing yet? The behaviors we were taught as good manners as little girls were really just us giving up our feelings about what made us feel uncomfortable for the sake of other people's feelings. But what about our own? When my oldest daughter was little, we were leaving a little league football game she was cheering at. When we were walking out to our car, a boy from the team came up behind her and put his arm around her and said something to her. Jade yelled in his face, "Ewwww, get off of me," and shoved him. At the time I remember I thought, "Oh no, Jade is a mean girl and probably hurt that boy's feelings." Really? Really? That young man put his arm around my daughter, and she responded with how she felt because she was uncomfortable, and I was embarrassed and felt bad for the boy?? That's crazy.

Can we please normalize the young girls in our lives speaking up for themselves and expressing when they aren't OK with something and make that OK? We need to break this cycle and teach the next generation of girls that they should trust their instinct and feelings, especially when they feel uncomfortable.

That is the root of why a lot of women allow inappropriate behavior and things to happen in their future because they haven't been taught how to respond when they feel uncomfortable for the sake of someone else's feelings.

> *Side note: Just for the record, I need to put this here because although this book is written specifically for women, if you're a man reading this—especially if you're a man in a supervisory role—and you have a woman who works with or for you that you act inappropriate toward and the woman laughs it off or makes light of it but never initiates a complaint, SHE DOESN'T LIKE YOU, and what you're doing is sexual harassment. Stop being gross and creepy. She may act nice, but you're her boss, so what the hell other choice does she have? She's probably been conditioned to hide her discomfort for the sake of her job.*

Anyway, ladies, as I was saying, these responses are conditioned in us very early and lead to behaviors as we're older that cause us to not trust ourselves in truly knowing what it may be that we want or think is best. We were taught to never trust ourselves or our reactions. We don't know what we want to eat; we only feel that we shouldn't. We don't feel we can be tired when there are still things to do; we only know we need to get them done. We aren't allowed to feel comfortable in our own skin, only to know that we're too big, little, shouldn't wear this or that, too old for this, but too young to do that.

We don't know our real hair color because we've been dying it since we were 14. We get Botox, buy new wardrobes, purchase name brands because others say they're "in." We act how we think we should act when in a meeting at work and say what we think others want to hear and second guess every good thought. We replay girls' night conversations the next morning, overanalyzing everything we said in fear that we said something we shouldn't have or sounded dumb. We look to others to validate the things we know to be true.

We compare, we negative self-talk, we beat ourselves up over and over for being ourselves. It's so sad. But it's all rooted in a lack of self-trust that was programmed into us from the time we were born. We're terrified of doing something wrong. We don't want to offend, ruffle feathers, or risk criticism. This is so deeply ingrained, carved, and branded in a woman's soul that she can't even feel the instantaneous way she pulls herself out of whatever equation she's in.

It's no wonder we can't trust ourselves enough to take action and be brave when called to be. Studies have even shown that women have more difficulty making decisions than men. An article by Ilan Shrira on scientificamerican.com says that new research suggests that gender plays a role in decisions because men tend to organize the world into distinct categories whereas women see things as more conditional and in shades of gray.

Psychologists at the University of Warwick had men and women judge how each of 50 objects fit into a certain category— whether it belonged, did not belong, or only partially (some-what) belonged. For example, is a cucumber a fruit? Is a horse a vehicle? After making each judgment, people reported how confident they were about their decision.

Men were more likely to see an object as fully belonging or not belonging to a category, while women more often judged that objects only partially belonged. As women, we tend to see more of the nuances in the overall picture, taking what is evident, and what is not, into each of our decisions. What was even more intriguing, though, was that men and women were equally confident about their decisions once they'd come to a conclusion. This means the gender difference wasn't due to men simply being more certain or women more uncertain about their judgments. Instead, it suggests men and women perceive the world differently.

This may happen for a couple of reasons. One possibility is that societal gender roles promote more absolute, black-and-white views in men and more detailed, complex views in women. Traditionally, cultures have rewarded males for being decisive and proactive, even if it means jumping to conclusions. In contrast, females are socialized to be more thoughtful and receptive to others' views, even if it means being more self-critical. This socialization not only affects behavior and personality; it also colors our perceptions. For instance, women perceive greater risk across many real and hypothetical scenarios relative to men, partly because risk-taking is a central and esteemed component of the masculine gender role.

So as women, we can shy away from risk-taking, aka brave acts, because we're conditioned to overthink, over process, and over worry about the implications of the decisions we're making. But what's interesting is that studies have also shown that women tend to have better instincts than men. An article in "Professional Security Magazine" states that a woman's intuition goes deeper than cultural gender expectations. On a biological level, women have increased brain activity as well as greater blood flow in areas of the brain that control memory and emotion, which could explain why women exhibit more intuition than men.

The problem is that, as I mentioned earlier, although scientifically we have the intuition and the ability to make decisions based on a broader scope of understanding, our ability to trust ourselves in decisions can be impacted because we've been rewired to make sure that what we do pleases others. Our environments and people in our lives can impact what we do and how we do it, thus creating more nuances and questions within a single decision.

Then how do we step out of ourselves and apply the Missy Elliot technique to this? (Remember: Put that thing down, flip it and reverse it.) You must first understand that you can't change a lifetime of wiring to feel or think a particular way overnight. But I have some good news for you. If you've gotten this far in the book, you've already started the transformation. In order to start building trust in yourself, you have to (really) understand your *who*—your values, your boundaries—and your *why*—what's important to you. Reconnecting with yourself and listening to your own needs as it relates to decision-making that is truly rooted in who you are and your impact why will move you out of where you are and into a life of fulfillment.

Remember:

Why Power > Will Power

You've tapped into your why power by identifying your impact why. Your stories and experiences have defined your why. So, afraid or not, you can't compromise on that. You have no other choice but to just brave it.

In moments of doubt, if you reflect back to your impact why— the real impact you want to make and why you want to make it—then even if you're afraid, you can have confidence knowing that your decision is in alignment with your why and it will give you the boost you need in order to be brave.

So...

Breathe. Embrace fear. Trust yourself.

And in times of doubt, whisper to yourself...

"I'm just gonna brave it."

Reflect before you Neglect.

Write here:

What are you afraid of that's keeping you from living a fulfilling life?

. . . .

. . . .

. . . .

. . . .

. . . .

How does understanding who you are and your *"Impact why"* give you the confidence to just brave it?

. . . .

. . . .

. . . .

. . . .

. . . .

CHAPTER EIGHT:

"I'm Just Gonna Brave It"

I was a little under a half year into my journey with the Women's Leadership Circle, an all-female mastermind group in my industry led by a dear friend of mine, Amy O'Connor, when she found out she had stage four cancer. Finding out at stage four is pretty intense, as you can imagine. Every day can make a huge difference in progress toward healing or setbacks. Amy, as she does with all things, battled her sickness like none other. She was a national sales trainer by trade. I always referred to her as the Michael Jordan of sales training. But after watching her battle cancer for over a year, I realized she is really the Michael Jordan at life.

After her diagnosis, she was thrown full into the trenches of every possible treatment that she was eligible for. This threw a bit of a wrench into life, as treatment became her number one priority and how these treatments made her feel varied day by day. As we approached our women's leadership circle session in August, although she was determined to lead the session, she knew that leading a full-day session might be tough, so she asked me and another woman to cover two of the segments.

I was honored to be asked and wouldn't dare say no, as I wanted to support her in any way possible during this time. But between you and me, the idea of speaking to and leading this group of powerhouse women leaders was daunting, to say the least. I had created foundations of friendships with these individuals, but I didn't feel validated in my ability to teach them anything, much less feel worthy of leading them. Why would they trust me or listen to anything I had to say? But in true Amy Druhot fashion, I figured I would say yes and just brave it until I made it.

I only had a couple of weeks to prep and didn't have a lot of free time, so I desperately needed inspiration to pull together last-minute content on "how we lead others," Then on the afternoon of July 25, 2022, life, as it often does, handed me what at the time felt like one of the most embarrassing moments of my life. But the laughter and the lessons that have come out of that story have been some of the most impactful in my life.

You've heard the phrase, "Your mess becomes your mission"? No statement could ever be truer.

It was a Monday after a busy weekend. If your Mondays are anything like mine, they're filled with nonstop meetings and leftover requests from the weekend. (Being in new home sales, my team works weekends, so I start my week with a page-long to-do list to complement the back-to-back meetings already scheduled for me. By the end of the day, I typically feel exhausted.

Lucky me, on top of the endless to-do list and meetings, my weekend was so busy that I didn't have time to make it to the grocery store. I had no other choice but to go on my way home after work because my kids have this annoying habit of having to eat dinner...like every day. They're entitled. What can I say? I blame my husband for this, because, well, that's what we do. (Right, ladies?)

To make matters worse, we'd gone through a period of time in Virginia where it was two weeks of rain almost daily and that day of all days was the day that they were calling for the worst of it. And in the words of the great Missy Elliot, "I can't stand the rain." But I checked the radar before leaving work and although it was close, it looked like if I walked out the door right at 5 p.m. and strategically raced through the store like I was on "Supermarket Sweep," I might, just might, get out in enough time to miss the rain.

Clock hit 5 and I slung my backpack and purse over my shoulder and walked toward the door. As I walked past my division president's office and said goodbye, I heard the words we all cringe to hear when in a hurry... "Oh, Amy, question real quick before you leave." I did my best to listen intently to his question so I could respond quickly and precisely with no room for additional questions, trying hard to ignore the anxiousness I felt building inside of me. I took tiny baby steps toward the door as I answered him. Mouth was responding calmly, but body language showed an urgency to leave. I responded and paused, to which he replied, "Sounds good. See you tomorrow." Yes! Mission accomplished with only a few minutes lost, still on track to avoid the rain. Rain: 0. Amy: 1.

I decided that although Wegmans is more popular than most other grocery stores, it was the best option because Wegmans is my jam. I know exactly where each item on my list is located without hesitation so I would spend less time locating the items and could get in and out quickly. As I was driving to the store, I could see the dark clouds begin to roll in. But I was still feeling pretty good about my odds. The radar I checked 30 minutes before leaving the office showed the storm over Wegmans at 5:34, which was better than Food Lion, which was a little further west, at 5:23. Wegmans is nine minutes from my office, so even though I pulled out of the parking lot at 5:07, I expected to arrive at Wegmans by 5:16, which gave me 18 minutes to get in, grab what I needed, and make it back out to the car before the rain. I had this down to the minute. Rain: 0 Amy: 2.

I pulled into the parking lot at 5:16 on the dot. (I felt like I should give myself an extra point for the yellow/reddish light I went through on the way to make this happen, but not sure traffic violations earn points.) And to be honest, I was feeling pretty good about myself at this point. I hustled through Wegmans like I was competing for the gold in the Olympics in speed walking, aka racewalking.

And the race begins. Amy Druhot is off to a great start as she rounds the corner past the produce section. Her strategy is not one we've seen before, actually passing the produce items on her list as she heads to the meat section first. She passes the hot bar in record speed, not even slowing down to glance at the premade charcuterie she often purchases despite it never being on her list. Looks like she's on her way to the chicken, and would you look at that, she grabs a bag from overhead for her meat without even stopping. Trusting completely that the metal hook that grabs the hole to rip the bag will hit just right... is she right?? Will the bag rip effortlessly?....yyyyyeeesssss.... aaaand she does it, my friends. That was one perfect tear technique if I ever saw one!

The crowd is going wild as she makes her way back to the produce. I see what she did here; she's using a predetermined route working from the outside of the store for efficiency. She doesn't slow down as she grabs the lettuce, the tomatoes, the cucumber. This girl is on fire! She heads toward the canned goods aisle and grabs the garbanzo beans and croutons like it's nobody's business. Are the bottom of her heels made of rubber? Because she's burning it!!! She's coming around the last turn as she heads toward the finish line (aka checkout line). When...what's this... she rolls right past them... what's happening... ooooohhhhh noooooo, she forgot the a-vo-cado! What is she going to do? I can't take the anticipation; I'm on the edge of my seat. She swings back past the produce and grabs an avocado without even pushing in the end to make sure it's ripe.

Keeping her priorities straight...quantity of time over quality of product. Can't say I blame her there. Can she make up the lost time as she heads back toward the finish line (aka checkout line)? With moments to spare...Can. She. Do. It?.... SHE DOES!! I wouldn't think it was possible it I didn't see it for myself but Amy Druhot has just set a new world record and won the gold for her performance in grocery store racewalking. Rain: 0 Amy: 3.5 (Gave myself a half point for the traffic violation.)

I checked out despite my avocado setback and headed out toward the exit with 3 minutes to spare until 5:34. Remember a few minutes ago when I said I was feeling good about myself? No, NOW, I was feeling really good about myself. Confidence was oozing from every pore as I turned the corner toward the exit when...

The exit doors opened.

And the wind slapped me in the face like Will slapped Chris. Despite my planning and near perfect execution, the underdog had come back for the win. Rain 1,000,000,000,000,000. Amy 3.5.

This downpour was unlike anything I'd ever seen before. It was like the tears of ten thousand women when Ricky Martin announced he was gay. The rain was moving horizontally across the parking lot at speeds that far surpassed my racewalking record and at about three inches deep on the surface. I walked out in disbelief as I stood under the overhang with around 12 other individuals who'd also just lost to the rain. We stood there, as we all do in these moments, awkwardly making eye contact with each other, shaking our heads as we each debated internally on what we should do.

As I debated with myself, I started trying to assess the nuances, as we women do, within the situation. Playing out all possible scenarios. I mean, despite the wall of rain, I could make out my black SUV about 25 yards in front of me with no other vehicles in the way. I reached inside my purse and pulled out my keys to see if I could unlock it from where I was standing. "Click, click." It worked. I only had two brown bags to carry and I could easily leave the cart and carry the bags to the car. So, I had a clear shot, could carry the bags, and my car was unlocked but I was still not convinced that I was going to make a run for it.

I looked to my right and made eye contact with a woman standing next to me who shrugged and then I looked to my left. There was a man standing there—a big burly man. I like to think of him as the antihero of the story. (I'm the hero, of course). He was broad-shouldered, bald, and he was wearing a t-shirt, basketball shorts, and tennis shoes. I watched him for a second and I realized he was debating whether or not he was going to go out in the rain. In my mind I was like, "Oh, man, up, dude. It's water!" I was literally standing there in a white blouse, blue linen slacks, and heels (with hair extensions, I must add) and I was considering it, but this "man" wasn't?!?

I don't know what came over me but in that moment, I heard a voice in my head that said, "Oh, no, no, no, no, no. I'm about to show these people how it's done."

One thing you've learned about me by now is that when I do something I not only do it, but I want credit for doing it. I like a parade, remember? So, I decided in that moment to make eye contact with all 12 people standing under the overhang and then announce loudly...

"I'M JUST GONNA BRAVE IT"

As if they all were actively anticipating what the lady in the white blouse was going to do. And because I wanted them to all be watching me as I heroically showed them how a woman does it.

I stepped out into the rain and as my first foot settled down into the three inches of water on the surface (which by memory feels like I was in slow motion), I instantly knew that I had made the wrong decision.

You see, I may seem bougie at times but deep down I'm just a Target girl. And on that particular Monday I was wearing a pair of heels from Target. Let's be honest. If I was wearing Louboutins, I would have just waited until next spring. But Target heels felt rain appropriate. These heels to be exact:

Now, what Target doesn't tell you when you purchase these shoes (and sensibly they should add a warning label to the box) is that when you add water to the shoe, they instantly become two personal slip 'n slides. And not slip 'n slides that move in the same direction. My feet immediately started slipping all over the place in all different directions. The only logical thing I could think to do was not turn around and go back under the overhang—I mean I couldn't turn back after just announcing to everyone that I was going to brave it—but was to keep my feet moving in the general direction of the shoe. Which also meant my legs would need to follow suit. So, there I was, walking through a river of a parking lot, with horizontal rain slapping me in the face, with a crowd of 12 watching me "show them how it's done," while my legs looked like a baby giraffe doing a Riverdance routine when trying to walk for the first time. I keep thinking about what it must have looked like from behind as they were all watching me. Not to mention I was wearing a WHITE BLOUSE—didn't think that one all the way through. AND, I wear clip-in hair extensions daily and I guess the extensions are not only heavy but water-resistant because my real hair was whipping around like a tornado on top of my head but I could feel my hair extensions lying flat.

Just when I thought it couldn't get any worse, my right foot must have slipped a little too high up the shoe and my foot came out of the bottom strap. So now my shoe was hanging on solely by the upper strap and my shoe had shifted sideways and I was limping with the ball of my foot literally walking on the water-engulfed pavement. The only logical thing (there goes my logical thinking again that's been so helpful to me so far), but the ONLY logical thing I could think to do in that moment was to "flick" the shoe to try to get it back onto my foot. But when I flicked the shoe, I don't know if it was the adrenaline, or the wind, but I kicked the shoe about 20 feet in the air. I kept thinking about how the crowd of people watching must have been verbalizing with their hands over their mouths "oh," "oh," "Ooohhhh" through each phase and when the shoe flew through the air, they must have thought in that moment, "This lady has gone crazy. Why did she just kick her shoe off?"

I ran over to grab the shoe, all the while my hair was still whipping and my one shoe and leg were still doing the "wobble, wobble, come on and shake it, shake it" dance. And as luck would have it, as I was running, one of my bags of groceries ripped open. And you know that feeling when one little thing from the bag starts to go, and you need to adjust but when you do, something else starts to slip. And before you know it, it's a slow-motion train wreck? Yep, you got it. Tomatoes and the can of garbanzo beans spilled out on to the ground. Oh, and at this point the shoe was still airborne; it hadn't even touched down yet.

I scraped up my groceries, my shoe, and what little dignity I still had left and made my way to my car, run-limping the last 15 feet or so. Finally, I had made it safe and sound. Slightly traumatized, but safe and sound.

I took a selfie to send to Amy O'Connor with the caption, "Just wait until I tell you what just happened to me." And now for your viewing pleasure...

I love how in the photo you can actually see that my hair extensions are still dry. What's also great is my hair is as straight as a pencil naturally, so the tornado wind gave me the perfect beach wave. (Looking for the positives.)

The best part was after I got in the car and sent the text, before I could even pull out of the parking spot...

IT. STOPPED. RAINING.

And my crowd of 12, bald burly man included, all walked calmly and dry out to their cars. There was nothing I could do but just sit up tall and drive confidently as I pulled out of the parking lot.

I "just braved it" all right. And I did, in fact, show those people how it was done.

But that's life, right?!? When we brave things, it's often things that no one else is willing to do. Sometimes it's something that no one else has ever done. And it's messy and ridiculous and embarrassing. But it's not meant to be perfect. When we brave things, we're often setting a path for those who come behind us. Showing them how to brave it (or in this case, how not to). But being afraid and not knowing the outcome but doing it anyway is the true definition of being brave. So, in the moments when you need to step out in the rain or set a path to show others how it's done, or to follow your instinct and do things to create a fulfilled life aligned with your impact why and you don't know where to start, announce out loud to yourself and those around you...

"I'M JUST GONNA BRAVE IT"

CHAPTER NINE:

Oh, No, She Didn't

But, yes, she did.

"Just brave it" may have been a phrase I proclaimed for the first time in the Wegmans parking lot. And the comedic story that surrounds it may seem silly in comparison to the things I've braved in life. But that's the magic of it.

Sometimes just braving it is taking a step out into the storm in front of an audience who witnesses your life's most awkward moment and sometimes it's something entirely different. But embracing the phrase can not only give us confidence in moving past our fears in the future; it can also help us to see all that we've overcome in the past.

I asked women I knew from all over the country to share with me their "Just Brave It" stories to give more examples of how other women choose to "brave it" in life. One of the most interesting findings in this request was that almost every woman who responded started by saying "I don't consider myself to be very brave." (over and over) Then they would look into their past and share the most amazing story of bravery. I was humbled and inspired by each story I received, and I'm sure you will be too.

Here are a collection of stories from other women who "Just Braved It." I hope it inspires you to look into your past and acknowledge the times when you, too, were brave. I also hope that when faced with adversity in the future, you can remind yourself of how capable you are and choose in those moments to "Just Brave it."

These are real stories from real women and are powerful narratives from some of their most challenging moments. Some of these stories dive into raw and intense experiences, making them poignant reads. If you find the stories emotionally demanding, it's perfectly OK to consider skipping this chapter for now. Some may find inspiration in revisiting these stories later, while others may feel compelled to just brave it and immerse themselves into these narratives immediately. The choice to engage in this section is entirely yours, allowing for a personalized, inspired, and meaningful read.

———————————

Chelsea T. – In 2020, I found myself in a position of being pursued by another company. I was happy at my current job, and thought I'd be there forever. I called myself a "lifer" there, and I definitely drank the Kool-Aid. However, the dangling carrot of a VP role NOW vs. waiting for that role to come along at my current company was a tough inner dialogue. I did all of the deep internal work and realized that I could just brave it and jump NOW, or I could wait seven to eight years for the person above me in rank to retire. Seven to eight years. That's a long time. That's an entire market cycle. A lot can happen in this industry in seven to eight years. A downturn. An acquisition. A merger. A change in guard. I could wait and be comfortable in the natural progression that my company chose for me or I could just brave it, push through the imposter syndrome, and go for it. I chose the latter, although it was mentally, personally, and professionally very tough. I felt like I was letting my team down because I was the head cheerleader of our company culture and had just onboarded new employees, telling them about how I'd be a "lifer" at this company. At the end of the day, I decided that "selfish" shouldn't be a bad word. Selfish by definition means: "lacking consideration for others; concerned chiefly with one›s own personal profit or pleasure." That sounds bad at first. But I broke it down and realized that if I wasn't chiefly concerned with my own profit, pleasure, advancement, and growth—who else would be? Deciding to brave it has been the best decision of my life and the discomfort, imposter syndrome, and "being a beginner again" has opened more doors than I could have ever imagined.

Tonya K. – When I was 16 years old, I was living in a hotel efficiency with my mom and stepdad because my stepdad had, once again, spent all of our money on drugs and we had been evicted from yet another apartment complex. I was lost, embarrassed, depressed and, quite frankly, had decided to give up. The moment I had the pills in my hand was the scariest moment of my life to date and I'm now 42. I sat in that dirty bathroom and realized I had a choice. I could take the pills and it all would go away OR I could "just brave it" and I could change my circumstances. The next day I told my mom I was moving out. I left that hotel room behind, moved out on my own, graduated high school, got married, have two beautiful children and an amazing career that I love. I gave myself the gift of a whole life, all because I chose to "just brave it."

Anonymous — I wasn't sure that I'm as brave as I am stubborn, persistent, and driven. I'm so driven to achieve my goals that I forget to be afraid, honestly. Just brave it to me means not letting the trauma in my past impact my success; instead it drives me forward. However, I still grapple with old images, feelings, and beliefs about myself fostered by childhood trauma. That's been my ongoing life struggle in learning to love myself and truly implement self-care at the core level. I will win, succeed, push myself, and go for the "gold" every time relentlessly. I will protect and fight and stand up for my people even when I lose myself doing so. It's taken me most of my life to get where I am in loving myself and it's ongoing, with a lot to accomplish. I have a long way to go to truly let go of old thoughts, beliefs, anger, and behaviors and I work daily on it. But this I know is true—while I still make poor choices or react—I am resilient, I am powerful, and I do not give up no matter how bad I feel. I push forward and bravely try to face each day working to be a better version of myself than before. I don't always succeed, as I am my worst critic with echoes of "it's not enough" and fearful of being "exposed for my true self" permeating my professional and personal life. But I get up and find a way to move forward with laughter, love, a huge heart, and kindness. I remind myself as many people and authors have famously written, "That was then; this is now." I work valiantly daily to find my peace.

Abby C. – It had been three years of trying to get pregnant. I went for yet another checkup with my reproductive endocrinologist. I had already had surgeries and multiple procedures. I'd been poked and prodded for years. I was sure his next step was going to be IVF. As I sat in the sterile medical office, the doctor's advice was not what I expected. He said, "I don't recommend IVF because I don't think it will work. I don't think you will carry your own child." My stomach sank, the tears started. My husband wasn't with me, as this was supposed to be a routine appointment, not a life-changing conversation. Before I knew it, there were two nurses in the room and this team of people I barely knew telling me about adoption and therapy. I felt like they were trying to put a Band-Aid on a very fresh and deep wound. I broke free of that office as quickly as I could and sat in my car, devastated. My heart was breaking. All the dreams I saw for a family that once were a clear picture instantly became a jumbled pile of puzzle pieces. I didn't know what to do. All I knew was that I felt very called to be a mom and I couldn't imagine a future without kids. I couldn't shake the vision I once had and I wasn't about to give up on it after one doctor telling me no. I sought a second opinion. This doctor's advice was a one-two punch. Not only did he reiterate I would likely not have kids, but he also highly recommended I get a hysterectomy, and quickly. He said it would increase my qualify of life. Nothing about permanently giving up my ability to carry children felt like an enhancement to my life. That was my first and last visit with that doctor. Over the next year, my husband and I explored adoption and fostering. Although they're both wonderful ways to build a family, I still felt like there wasn't enough proof as to why I couldn't carry a child. I refused to give up on my dream. I found a magnet one day that said WAIT. HOPE. EXPECT. I put it on my fridge and every day I committed to having patience, not losing hope, and expecting if I had a dream and I felt this was for me, then it was. Then one day I got an email from a new reproductive clinic. They had actually bought out my first doctor's office. They boasted about having NEW technology and a 100% IVF guarantee program, if you qualified. I read and reread that email probably five times before I showed it to my husband. We decided no harm could be done in meeting with the new team of doctors and getting a third opinion. We went into that appointment with guarded optimism. As we sat in yet another doctor's office reviewing our charts and lab work, I was waiting for the same news. I was expecting him to say, "You don't qualify." But to our surprise he started reviewing the IVF process and why he thought it was our best option. He started reviewing percentage chances and what unique type of IVF we needed to do. And I paused him and said, "Wait, do you think we qualify for this? You think it can work?" And he said "Yes!"

That day started the physically and emotionally challenging journey that is IVF. After I failed one round of IVF, another retrieval, three transfers, and a miscarriage, I got pregnant and gave birth to our miracle, Cecily. And with only one frozen embryo remaining, I got pregnant a second time with yet another beautiful baby girl, Lucy. Each step of the way I knew what I wanted. I reached more than my fair share of roadblocks. I didn't change the dream; I just had to adjust the path. I had plenty of reasons to give up. Fear set in more days than I would care to admit. But courage won. I am so grateful that I just braved it!

Sascha E. – Last year I had an idea, a new concept that I thought would really succeed if I could find a way to get it to market. Getting an investor on board wasn't the hardest part. The most difficult thing for me was that I knew it would take a lot of learning (see also: making mistakes) to start this new passion project.

Working through design details, negotiating pricing, handling missed deadlines and sizing challenges provided headaches that had me wondering if I had the grit to see it through. And that was all before figuring out how to set up an online store and advertising to sell my first item!

I knew I had to push through the fear of setbacks and failure and muster the courage to overcome the trepidation that could stall this dream.

Brianna Wiest inspired me with this: "I hope you know that a thousand failures are the building blocks of your becoming. I hope you are not dissuaded by the dead ends; I hope you know that they are not final destinations. I hope you know that it is the courage to keep beginning that ultimately gets us all to where we are meant to be."

It can be intimidating to take the leap, but I realized I could lean into the reality that it's just as risky to let it pass you by. What if we get exactly what we want when we push through and brave the challenges? I believe that's a chance worth taking.

Nicole C. – As a new-ish mom working full time, I often come across moments that I'm not prepared for or that throw me for a loop. Let's be real—motherhood is unpredictable! When you add in a full-time job that you're so passionate about and love so much, balance between the two is tricky.

Recently, the flu hit our household. I was taking care of two sick kiddos all while trying to work remotely. My husband is in education so he doesn't have the flexibility I do. I managed to schedule an important ZOOM meeting while both kiddos napped. Well, here's where unpredictability comes in! My 1.5-year-old daughter awoke from her nap sooner than typical. She was crying in the background, and I wanted to stay present for this important call. I thought to myself, it's OK, you can do this. Grab your daughter and stay on mute. Just Brave It. Do BOTH. I quickly shut off my camera, grabbed my daughter and some fruit snacks, and turned my camera back on. She LUCKILY sat there so patiently and, of course, hammed it up in front of the camera, making for a fun interaction on the other end. I truly felt like a multitasking super-woman after that unpredictable moment. "Just Brave It" to me, means staying calm and strong in unpredictable moments!

Noelle G. – At 31 I found myself running in the middle of the night from a 7 year marriage. The escape was unplanned and reactionary. For reasons I won't get into, I could no longer stomach the idea of living with the man I had planned so many dreams around and, inadvertently become entirely dependent on. Sure, I had earned a degree in Interior Design and worked for a brief period in the field. But for the better part of the 7 years we had shared the bulk of my energy had been invested in him and his dream. It wasn't until the reality began to set in weeks later that I was neck deep in quick sand. Because I ran, I wasn't allowed back in my home. Because I ran, I wasn't allowed back into our business, better yet, my income. I was literally alone, with the clothes on my back with no home of my own and no way to support myself. Luckily I did have a family to cover me while I figured out my next steps. As the weeks ticked by I got an attorney but all he really managed to do was uncover some hefty tax evasion that had my name all over it (never be too trusting) and hammer out a deal that cut me loose from any debt that I may have to carry away. But that was it. A home in the country club was gone. A beautiful restaurant that had my blood, sweat and tears all over its soul was gone. The whole life that I had been working on and all those dreams were gone. Oh, it seems worth mentioning that, during that 7 years I was deemed infertile. So motherhood was gone. The next few months were dizzying. A lot of isolation. A lot of tears. A lot of praying. A lot of spinning out. Then one day a friend was talking about a designer in town that we both knew that had been working with a company designing model homes for new home construction. Apparently, this designer was in a bind and couldn't deliver on some of her obligations. Would I be willing to jump in and do the heavy lifting of installing a model? It would require traveling. Hell yeah! Get me outta here!

A week later I landed in a remote area of Texas. This was before Google maps and we had spent a solid 3 hours with our paper map finding this new community. We got our lay of the land, checked out the 3200 square foot home and headed to our hotel. I had a little info on what to expect. Some pictures of the furniture pieces that had been selected, as well as artwork and accessories. The next morning on the drive to the model I was so excited. I felt like something wonderful was happening for the first time in so many months. The truck pulls up. Over the course of the next couple of hours enough "stuff" comes off the truck to fill up about a room and a half of this home. Where's the rest? Everyone is just looking at me. What the hell? I didn't plan this. I'm just here to style this place, I'm just here to execute. The person in charge looks at me and says "so what are you going to do?" I asked for a minute. Went to the bathroom and busted out in quiet tears. It didn't take long for me to decide that I was just going to have to buck up and brave it. I could do this. I walked out of the bathroom and found the sales person. "Where's the best place to find furniture around here?" I asked. With my trusty paper map and a suburban I struck out. For the next 2 days I drove back and forth from the shopping district to the model home. Once the suburban was full, I would go back to the model and drop off what I had purchased, then go back and shop more. Once the stores closed, I began styling. All night long for two straight nights. I literally did not sleep for 3 days. When I finished I was so tired I couldn't even tell if it looked nice or not. I honestly didn't have the energy to care. I went to my hotel and crashed. After about 6 hours of sleep, I had my first shower in 3 days. God it felt good. I ventured back to the model to meet with the decisions makers from the builder. When I walked in I felt an enormous since of pride. Damn good work if I do say so myself. But, it wasn't up to me. After an hour and a half of walking room to room telling the story of the fictional family that I had designed this home for the builder loved it.

20 years later I sit writing these words as the President of my own interior design firm completing nearly 100 model homes annually. I am able to provide employment to up and coming designers and mentor them. Don't be fooled. There have been some really tough times over the course of the past 20 years and I have found myself in more bathrooms with eyes full of more tears. But since

that bathroom in Texas, I have never wondered if I have the ability to persevere. I know no matter what comes, I will just brave it. P.S. I am also now 16 years happily married with 2 boys (15 & 12).

Anya C. – Braving it was embedded in me from an early age when my family immigrated to the U.S. from Russia and I had no choice but to brave the unknown. Looking back, some of my biggest growth moments came from pushing past fear. Starting my podcast in 2018 felt terrifying and risky. Podcasting was still new, and mine was the first in the new home industry, so putting myself out there felt vulnerable. My biggest fear was judgment. What would people think? I was afraid, but as George R.R. Martin wrote, "The only time a person can be brave is when they are afraid." Had I let fear win, I wouldn't have made the impact I did on those meant to hear it. The podcast set me on a path that led me to where I am today. I had to silence the inner critic and just brave it.

Ashlee N. – In 2023, I set a goal to hike Angels Landing in Utah, which is rated one of the most dangerous hikes in the world. The ground is as slick as the climb is steep, with safety chains to hold onto to prevent people from falling off the edge. I've been terrified of heights for as long as I can remember but got sick of feeling gripped by fear and prevented from doing what I loved. Given the popularity and danger of the hike, I had to apply for a permit and was lucky to get my chance last April. As I made my way up the rim and watched the trail thin out ahead of me, I took a deep breath and "Braved It" across the cliff. It was terrifying, but beneath that fear was a bedrock of determination. It was the most rewarding day of my life! (until I fainted, then puked on some random stranger when I got to the bottom. Ha-ha!)

Rachea P. — My Just Brave It story has nothing to do with my professional life. But any time I recall it, or share it with others, it still feels as raw and real as the day I experienced it. I can still feel the tingling in my hands and the way my heart was pounding, and the dizzying surge of adrenaline as I made a choice that redefined my whole life.

On July 14, 2011, I went in for a routine sonogram. I was about 19 weeks along in my pregnancy, and I was relieved to see a tiny body with tiny arms and legs pop into view on the grainy screen of the machine. Hope filled me as I listened to the little beating heart. My previous pregnancy had ended in a traumatic miscarriage followed by a battle with guilt and depression. But this baby was going to be different—I knew it, I could feel it. This baby was healthy and alive and I would be able to bring it into the world.

My optimism at seeing the baby didn't last long. The previously chatty nurse turned the screen out of my view and began making rapid punches of keys. "So, is your husband coming today?" she asked, in the guise of small talk. "Yes, he was just running a little late," I said. "Let me go check and see if he's here for you," she said. And she abruptly walked out of the exam room, leaving me on the table with my belly still coated in gel. My intuition instantly began screaming the alarm. I knew something was off. Time seemed to draw itself out as I fought off dark memories. After fifteen minutes ticked by, I was beginning to entertain ludicrous scenarios: Did she forget about me and go on her lunch break? Has everyone left for lunch? Had there been a fire drill? Am I the only one here right now? Unable to stand my self-torment any longer, I got up and got dressed. My timing ended up perfect—as I stuck my head out the door of the exam room, the nurse was marching back with my OBGYN in tow. Confirmed. Something was wrong. I backed into the room as they entered. The nurse went to the sonogram machine and pulled up several images as the doctor explained to me that they had seen an abnormality in my baby. "Your baby has a cleft lip and palate," he said, indicating an area on the baby's face. My mental catalog rapidly fired off pictures of children I had seen with the condition. "Well, can't they fix that?" I asked stupidly, the news still taking root in my brain. "Yes, they can. But it's a hard, years-long reconstruction. And your sonogram shows a severe case. The baby won't be normal. And it's a sign that there are other possible birth defects." "Like what?" I pressed, trying to gain some footing on what he was trying to tell me. "Trisomy 13 for one—we'd do the testing, of course, but we have to hurry."

"Hurry?"

"Yes. You'll have to decide whether you want to terminate within the next week." I would have preferred being slapped. "We have a narrow window of opportunity to perform a procedure, considering that you're almost 20 weeks," he explained into my silence. "No." It was the only thing I managed to get out. I was shattered. My doctor continued to explain the birth defects that they would want to rule out with testing, the procedure of an amniocentesis, how long it would take to get results, needing weekly sonograms with a specialty clinic ... but I wasn't really paying any attention. Thankfully, my husband arrived in the midst of the explanation and became an anchor of logic to my imminent emotional implosion. We agreed to a plan for testing, set another appointment, and left the office. But things were not so harmonious in subsequent discussions of what we needed to do and what would happen next. My husband had leaned toward "trying again." He knew my career was stressful and time-consuming. He didn't want to see me sacrifice just to be heartbroken again. He'd seen that mess before. He was scared. My mother and grandmother echoed, "Don't bring that baby into the world; it's too hard. You'll have regrets." They were scared, too.

I felt alone and angry. The weight of a ticking clock seemed to loom over my head, demanding that I choose the fate of a life. I didn't like the options and I didn't like the odds. I didn't like being scared. And over the course of those conversations and reasonings, something else entirely was born in me: pure defiance. I chose to NOT be scared.

I decided I didn't want to give up on my baby. I didn't care what abnormality he or she would have. I had been chosen to carry this tiny soul, and if God willed it, then I would follow the natural course He set.

At my husband's and mother's insistence, I agreed to go through with the amniocentesis, cried through the whole of the procedure, and flat-out refused to talk to them about it afterward. "No," I said, more boldly and repeatedly than I'd ever done in my entire life. I began to feel empowered every time I said it. I secretly liked that I had left them all wondering where their agreeable, people-pleasing, perfection-seeking, and accommodating Rachea had gone. In her place was a new woman—and she was rebellious, contrarian, and taking the reins on her own life.

The test results came back, and they showed no signs of any further chromosomal abnormalities. But still, we were cautioned on the unknowns, the risks, and the needs of a child with our baby's condition. The doctor then asked me, "How do you want to proceed?". Without hesitation, I looked at him—and despite the feeling of jumping into open space without a net, knowing that I wouldn't know for sure exactly what I was getting myself or my baby into, knowing that I was going against everyone's advice and perfectly sane logic, knowing that I may have to sacrifice my career, knowing only that I didn't really know anything—I said boldly, "I'm having this baby." A few months later, Maverick entered the world. Quietly and calmly and perfectly. His complete bi-lateral cleft lip and palate (CBCLP) were indeed more severe than we could have anticipated. But we knew immediately that he would be a fighter. He hadn't needed NICU services and he figured out how to feed from an eye-dropper quickly. As they laid him on my chest for the first time, a feeling of absolute certainty and relief came over me.

I had been right to fight for this.

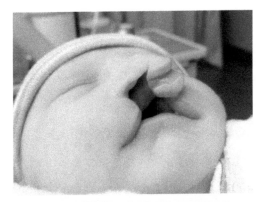

And I'll continue to fight... and defy the odds... and question the options... because his journey continues and we will be with him for every step of it.

Susan W. – My just brave it moment was deciding to let people close to me know (friends, family, and also co-workers) that one of my kids was changing her name and pronouns (possibly sexual identity at the time too) and that I was in support of it. Part of being brave was admitting to myself and those around me that I also might need help or accommodations sometimes as we had a lot to work through in order to support her mental health struggles. Before opening up, I knew that it would be OK. Still, it was a huge jump to get past the feelings of inadequacy as a mom, guilt of missing signs of the struggles, and concern that there would be more attention on my family and our struggles than what I wanted, which might change relationship dynamics or what co-workers felt I was capable of handling at work. But I just braved it. That was the most amazing feeling and part of it all. It helped me fully realize that I had chosen the right people to surround myself with and that I was capable of getting through it.

Alexa D. – Becoming a mom was the moment I just had to brave it. I know some women just jump into this with open arms, but I was TERRIFIED. Choosing to be a mom was really hard for me. It felt like I was standing at the top of cliff and everyone was telling me to jump. But I also felt in my heart that being a mom would bring new meaning to my life, I just wasn't sure what that looked like yet. Ultimately, I'm so glad I "jumped" because being a mom is the most fulfilling job. Wiley just lights up my life with so much joy and love.

———

Jamie H. – One of our employees, a young guy in his early 30s, died suddenly. There is strong suspicion that it was suicide, or perhaps more accurately, an unintentional suicide because of hard drugs. We don't know for sure nor will we ever. It was shocking to say the least, but what made it even more traumatic was that he's the LAST person you'd expect with any issues. The epitome of positivity. Just the most magnetic, dynamic, charismatic soul who absolutely radiated kindness and joy and positive energy.

He died on a Monday. That Friday, we were scheduled to have our annual company beach day, a time-honored tradition to which everyone looks forward every year. The exec team quickly realized that that party would not be appropriate, but I still urged the team to get together for our regular company meeting. Every fiber in my being screamed that, as difficult as this was, we needed to come together, honor him, and discuss the reality of the situation. It was obvious that our team, understandably, didn't feel entirely equipped to discuss this publicly, especially due to the sensitivity of the situation and the unknowns surrounding his death. The obvious assumption was that he killed himself, but we didn't know that for sure. There was strong suspicion of drug use the days leading up to it, but we also didn't want to cast that light unfairly either. I knew I needed to be the person on the team to speak up. I knew I had a responsibility to both him and to the rest of the company to address the issues head on, but in a way that tackled mental health and death without unfairly insinuating what exactly transpired in this case.

In hindsight, I think it took a lot of boldness on my part, but at the time, I didn't think of it that way; I had a visceral reaction where I just knew to my core that I needed to step up to the challenge to help in any way that I could. I don't think it was until after my presentation at the company meeting that the magnitude of the situation really hit me. Even then, I'm not sure it really hit me, even as emails and texts of gratitude came in from my teammates... I think the biggest impact came when his wife reached out to me a few days later, saying she had the opportunity to watch the footage and that it was the first time she felt like she wasn't so alone.

It was in that moment that I fully understood that being brave, for me, wasn't really about me; it was about stepping up to help others in a time when they needed it. That then circles back to being about me in that my "why" ultimately leads back to making a difference; I want to be a difference-maker in this world. I need to serve a purpose beyond myself and leave this world a little better than I found it.

I learned acutely through this experience that bravery isn't always the stoicism by which it's often described; for me, bravery is about being openly vulnerable in a way that may help others.

Jennifer J. — I spent a lot of my life feeling like I wasn't good enough. There wasn't a particular event that led to this feeling that I can pinpoint, but I always had a sense that I wasn't pretty enough, smart enough, thin enough, or worthy enough of having the things that I wanted in life. Despite this, I persevered, finished college, and worked my way up in my first career in a male-dominated industry, being one of only three women in my position in the entire state. After being laid off from that job after six-and-a-half years, I found myself lost in figuring out what I wanted to do. I tried jobs and industries that I wasn't passionate about, trying to find inspiration but falling short. Despite this, I braved it and gave it my all, while keeping myself open to other possibilities. Through this experience, I found an industry that I was passionate about, but the company that I was with didn't see or foster my potential, sliding me back into thinking that I wasn't good enough. I once again found myself trying to find a job or career that I was passionate about and feeling that I wasn't meeting my potential or enjoying what I was doing enough. Through being brave and saying yes to things, I took the leap of uprooting my life and moving to Virginia. By nature, I'm very reserved and nervous around people that I don't know, and feel very awkward and unable to make conversation with new people. I braved it little by little to build a tribe around me at home. Talking to another mom at the bus stop led to being invited to a party, which led to being let into a tribe of women in my neighborhood, which I'd never had in my life. I said yes to leaving that first job that brought me to Virginia to one that would bring me to the Richmond market. I said yes to several more roles that were presented to me, even when I was nervous and had that self-doubt in my mind. I braved through bosses who didn't appreciate me, things I couldn't change due to bureaucracy, and co-workers who made me feel like I wasn't worthy of the roles I'd earned. I braved my nerves to attend events where I felt awkward and felt like people would judge me because I wasn't the conversationalist that I thought I should be. I braved being the only woman in the room and the self-doubt talking that I didn't deserve to be there. At one of these events that I talked myself into attending, I met someone who would change the trajectory of my career, introducing me to a wonderful group of women, many of whom I'd admired from afar but felt that doubt creeping in to be nervous to talk to. I found with this group of women that many of them had felt the same way that I did. Many of us have "imposter syndrome," but for what reason? We have all worked hard to get where we are, many of us while dealing with much more outside of work than our male counterparts. By braving it and saying yes to things that made me uncomfortable, I found my way back to a career that I loved where I feel appreciated, a neighborhood and location to live that I love, and a group of friends who have faced many of the same things that I have and lift me up every day, reminding me that I'm worthy of all that I desire, and continue to lend their bravery to me when I'm in need of a boost. Stepping into the uncomfortable and braving it can change the trajectory of your life. It did for mine.

Alexis B. – Bravery is a funny thing. I wouldn't consider myself a brave person. However, as I've tried to think of a time to write about here, I've found I don't give myself enough credit. I was 20 when I, an extreme homebody, decided to move from a small town in Texas to New York where I didn't know a soul within a 3 hour flight. I was 26 when I decided to go back to school to become a licensed optician. I was 29 when I was diagnosed with OCD and a depressive disorder where I had a hard time even getting in the shower or brushing my teeth. I was 31 when I decided to freeze my eggs because I am a carrier of Fragile X Syndrome and would likely have a child with special needs if I was to get pregnant naturally. I'm 33 now and was married last year, a month later I was laid off from my job and decided to start my own calligraphy business. Sometimes it feels like you're fighting to make it through another day, as if everything is happening to you but you're not making any choices for yourself. It's not until you take a minute to reflect do you realize you getting out of bed and brushing your teeth was brave. It was brave to give yourself injections so that you have the option to have a child later on. You were brave to start a new career path when the cards felt stacked against you. Bravery looks different in every stage of life and it's important to take the time to realize just how brave you are.

Kathy W. – Just brave it was a daily, if not maybe hourly, thing to say to myself when I was working in the medical field, though my job description really wasn't hard and I enjoyed the relationships with the patients. But I really had to just brave it with my supervisor because I was working for a woman who was worse than Meryl Streep, in "The Devil Wears Prada"!! She would never yell, always had a calm tone of voice, but before you knew it, she sliced you up and cut you down into nothing. It was always like a delayed effect that would just stick to you like glue for the rest of your shift. I began to realize that she was insulting me left and right! So I had to constantly just brave it. I couldn't afford to quit my job at the time. It paid very well and my husband was recovering from a work injury. But yet, I had to deal with this woman Monday through Friday. My just brave it became more of "It's not about me; it's about her." It was about her, projecting her stuff on all of us, so then my phrase changed to "Allow me to have Teflon skin to allow her toxic words to literally slide off of me and not ever be allowed to penetrate into my being!!" I would repeatedly pray for that, pictured me being covered with something so when she cut me down, it just slid off me and didn't affect me! You know, to this day, you can insult me to my face and be as mean and rude as you want. I know it's not about me and my Teflon skin is still strong and it just slides right off. So my just brave it turned into such a huge strength for me. Looking back on it now, it totally elevated me, but at the time it felt like hell.

Casie W. – In my first marriage, I was young and went through life like it was "supposed" to look. Meet someone, date the appropriate time, get engaged, plan the wedding, get hitched, and so forth. I had previously been in terrible relationships and never met anyone I could see would be a good partner. When I met my ex-husband, he was great on paper and truly is a great person. However, we just never were on the same page about anything. We had different political views, came from different backgrounds, I had student loans and he didn't, different religious backgrounds, and the list went on and on. Our differences made us both resentful and we harbored a lot of negative feelings and became more like roommates. I would watch Bravo in the bedroom and he would be watching sports in the den. Lying there, I would cry. I didn't recognize myself anymore and masked who I was to avoid arguments. I was lost. We had our daughter, Alley, in 2016 and she is my true angel on earth. As a mother, I would think about how her life would look with two parents always fighting or two parents who were happy. I was torn and constantly negotiated with myself, but I ultimately knew the decision I needed to make. I didn't want her to grow up thinking this was how a relationship should look and then continue the same cycle with a mismatched partner.

In the summer of 2018, I moved in with my parents and began the divorce process. Now anyone who has gone through or is currently going through a divorce, especially with children, knows it's so hard. I mean so hard! BUT, I was determined to make it as positive as I could. I focused on the entire reason I left, which was to be happy and love myself. I knew that by loving myself and being the best version of me, I would give my daughter the most precious gift in the world. That end goal kept me so focused on the "hard times." Now, nearly six years later, I can honestly say that my ex-husband and I are much happier people in our new lives. We each found significant others who complement us as humans and my child has two very loving homes, even though it's difficult for her. This is still good work because it created a space to invite healthier relationships. I put my needs aside and decided to have a great co-parenting relationship, because at the end of the day in this situation my daughter is the most important thing. This is daily work, but I believe even if you're not divorced, focusing on your child's mental health is so important. I've used it as an opportunity to become very close to her, talk about her fears and anxiety, and be extremely present with the time I have with her. In fact, this past summer we ALL (myself, her stepdad, father, stepmother, and her brother) went to Disney World together. Alley was in heaven, having everyone together for her, and we had an amazing time, despite Disney taking all of our money. I mean those Magic Bands are no joke! I'm aware that everyone's situation is very different on this topic, but the more I talk to people in a co-parenting situation, I realize many aren't willing to let go of their ego and do good work. My husband always says, "Do you want to be right or be happy?" and I couldn't agree more. I will always choose happiness.

─────────

Magda E. – Let me tell you about my journey. For over twenty years, I was at the top of the new homes sales game in Charlotte, North Carolina. Year after year, I was the best in the state, earning more than a million dollars annually. But deep down, I knew something was missing.

I always dreamt of doing more than just selling houses. I wanted to change people's lives, to help them see their true potential. So, after two decades in sales, I decided to make a big change. I took a chance and stepped into a new role as Vice President of Sales for Brookline Homes. This move was a huge leap for me. I went from being a star in sales to leading a team, focusing on their growth and success. At first, it was tough. I had to learn a lot of new things and adapt to a different way of working.

But as time went by, I started seeing the impact of my work. I was helping my team realize their talents and encouraging them to do their best. Seeing them grow and succeed brought me a joy I'd never experienced before. It was more satisfying than any sale I had ever made.

Through this journey, I learned a lot about myself and what truly makes me happy. It wasn't the money or the awards; it was helping others and seeing them thrive. My decision to pursue my dream brought me to a place of personal fulfillment and joy that I never knew was possible. And that's what really matters.

Cindy B. – I was married for 25 years to a brilliant, successful entertainment agent who became addicted to prescription drugs. After four years of dealing with this, I had to be brave and save myself. Leaving behind our home, fancy cars, traveling. Paying for my apartment and a mortgage. Every day wondering, is this the day we lose it all? That is, all material things!!! I still had my faith, health and myself!!! My life is very different now; this brave badass woman is more confident, closer to God, inspirational to others, and so grateful for the journey!!!

Shannon A. – It's always been my dream to play tackle football. As a tomboy growing up and watching football and hockey every weekend, I was able to play hockey as a kid, but never football. Fast-forward to my adult life, and being 100 pounds overweight just didn't lend itself to the fitness level needed to play, and there also weren't a lot of options for women to play football! Well, having lost 100 pounds and being in really great shape, I felt like I had missed the mark, because now I was 55 years old and too old to play football. And wouldn't you know, out of the blue, a woman saw me say something about wanting to play football on Facebook. She reached out to me and told me I wasn't too old, and that I should try out. She just happened to be the owner of a women's tackle football team in my town! So, I thought to myself, what have I got to lose? On a cold November morning, I pulled up to a football field where I didn't know anyone, in my tennis shoes and shorts, saying to myself "Just Brave It" as I got out of the car and walked over to the group of women, ready to try out! Lo and behold, I made the team!!! This just goes to show, go after what you want, you're never too old to chase your dreams, Just Brave It!!

Anonymous – When I was in my mid 20's I had just started my career in consulting sales. I was excited about the opportunity and embraced every moment. I quickly became known as the "up and coming star" of our department. We worked remotely so most of our meetings were via phone or video conferencing but on occasion my regional manager would visit when a client was coming into town. This particular visit I was not the one making the appointment. My manager called and said he had set an appointment with a potential new client, and he would be coming to town to meet with us. I was told to be at a trendy bar downtown at 6 and to dress to impress. I was there promptly at 5:55 dressed in black heels, black slacks, a black blouse and a black blazer. I felt sleek and definitely "to impress". My boss was there waiting for me at the bar. I asked him if we should get a table and he said we would wait there until the potential client showed up. 6:15...6:30... the client still not there. By 7:00 we were both on our third drink when I said," I guess this guy stood us up". My manager put his hand on my knee and looked me in the eye and said, "too bad for us I guess we will just have to make the best of my trip, you don't want me to have come all this way for nothing". I was shocked. I didn't know what to think or do, and I was pretty sure there was no "potential client". I excused myself from the bar and went to the bathroom and called my friend who told me no job was worth behavior like that. I asked a woman in the bathroom to tell my manager that I had asked her to let him know that I had gotten ill and had left. I was embarrassed and didn't know what more I could do. He called my phone 7 times that evening, I didn't answer. That next Monday we had our team call and I showed up. It was awkward but I still was not sure what I was going to do. But as soon as I got off that call I started applying for new opportunities. I left that job 2 weeks later, taking a $15,000 pay cut but I knew I needed just brave it and leave on principle. I am so glad I did. That job was temporary but opened up new opportunity that has led me to great success today. I am so glad I was brave enough to walk away from a situation that at the time terrified me. I didn't play the part and I stayed true to who I was. When I look back today the me now would have given him a good crotch punch before saying I quit and walking out the door. But I am proud of the 26-year-old version of me who found a way out and just braved it.

Mary W. – I was done. I was ready to call the airline and make reservations for my two small daughters—newborn and 2— and me to go back to my parents' home in another state.

My husband had retired from the military and taken a job as manager at a country club. He left home early, came home midday for a rest and then he returned to the club until any time from 10 pm to 1 am. He worked six days a week. On his day off he would play golf with the golf pro at different area golf courses.

We had only one car and we were living in a town where I did not know anyone. I was so lonely, so frustrated; and I had had enough.

Then, my husband walked in the door and told me that the club had chosen to accept his resignation—he had been fired! I could not walk away when he had just lost his job. I just could not take our family away from him too.

Shortly after, I found myself standing alone by my kitchen sink. To this day, I remember standing there so vividly. It was in that exact moment, at my wits end, that I knew I had to just brave it and so I turned to God. I remember saying, "God, I don't even know if you are real, but if you are and you can change me and change my marriage, you've got me from here on out."

I was not sure how, but life began to change as I began to live the commitment I made to God in that moment. I started going to church and I began to make friends, who are now lifelong friends. Everything was not easy. My husband was still the same man, but I was different. From that time, I chose to stay and work things out for another 36 years until my husband died several years ago. I learned to be wise in my interactions with him. The changes in me also made a difference for good in his life, too. We had the joy of bringing up our children together. I chose to just brave it and it brought me through to a better, easier life centered in Christ.

Brave is as brave does.

The bravery in these women's stories is evident. They are all inspirational, in the same way that your past stories are also inspirational. There is power not just in recognizing your brave moments but also sharing them with others. Bravery can be found in all forms, in our big moments and in the small, and when shared can not only inspire others but help us to just brave it in future moments of fear or hesitation.

I am so grateful that these women's stories are now a part of my story. And now that you have read them, they are a part of yours as well.

WHO +
WHY +
HOW =
Fulfillment

CHAPTER TEN:

Go Forth,
And Be Brave

According to "US News" in 2021, women made up only 31.7% of executive roles in the U.S. Why is this? Especially when research by Harvard Law Review showed that women outperform men in most leadership skills as it relates to taking the initiative, practicing self-development, driving for results, and displaying high levels of integrity and honesty.

I believe a lot of this has to do with our wiring. The not wanting to ruffle feathers, step on toes, or being afraid to speak up when we have value to add in fear of failure. We as women have too close a relationship with disappointment. The fear of disappointing others, of disappointing ourselves, and of just being disappointed in general. We're not born with this innate sense of disappointment, but over time, our hopes and expectations shift as we're told we need to please others above our own feelings (remember Chapter Seven), we're told we can't do something because we're girls, we're passed over in opportunities in life, and the expectation built by Disney movies <u>absolutely</u> is not a reality. Many women today are still assuming the traditional roles of the past—the children, errands, meal planning, cleaning—and yet many of us today also have careers. We feel a sense of disappointment almost daily in our expectations of wanting help from others but at the same time disappointment in ourselves for not feeling we have it all together and can get it all done. The feeling of fulfillment is almost impossible when you're filled with disappointment.

Remember the equation from earlier:

$$(Who) + (Why) + (How) = Fulfillment$$

Each part of this equation has equal importance when seeking a life of fulfillment. You can't truly have a sense of fulfillment without all three. Because without each, our disappointment default can kick in, leaving us with a sense of feeling let down and unfulfilled.

Who—If you don't have a true sense or understanding of who you are, your expectations for yourself are never clearly set. You can't recognize your strengths and weaknesses for what they are, accepting that we all have both, and you can feel disappointed by things and outcomes that were never meant for you in the first place. Without an understanding of who you are, you'll seek validation outward through comparison to try to discover this and will end up feeling unfulfilled and disappointed every time.

Why—Understanding your why, more importantly your impact why, gives you a sense of direction. It's a compass to keep you on track and a survival guide for when you get off track to help you find your way back. Understanding your why gives you purpose. Mayo Clinic studies have shown that those with a true sense of purpose live longer, sleep better, and have a more robust immune system, lower stress levels, and better cognitive function.

Having purpose also helps you to make better and quicker decisions as related to your why, making it easier to set boundaries for things that aren't aligned with your why. In general, having a clear purpose, an impact why, not only makes it easier to let go of disappointment but gives you a sense of happiness and fulfillment.

How—You may know who you are, and you may clearly know your why and the impact you want to make, but if you aren't doing anything to live a life centered in those things, you'll have no sense of fulfillment. Brave is an action. If you're not moving forward, setting boundaries, and stepping outside of your comfort zones, you'll feel a sense of disappointment even if you've defined what's important to you. Don't talk about it; be about it.

But how? If you looked at the lives of women living in their purpose with a true sense of who they are, you'll find a common theme: bravery.

But telling someone to "go forth and be brave" doesn't mean being brave should just come easily. Remember, I said I was good at being brave because I'm even better at being afraid. But when I'm afraid, I've gotten pretty good at just braving it.

With all things, the more you practice them, the easier and more natural they become.

So how then, do we start practicing bravery? Over the last few years, I've had the opportunity to not just discover my own path to living a brave life, but also to connect with women all over the country bravely living in their own purpose. In observing these women, I came to realize that being brave can mean a lot of things. It can mean having the strength to keep going, no matter how hard things get. It can mean standing up for your beliefs, even when they aren't the popular opinion. It can also mean taking risks, even when you're afraid and don't know the outcome. It can mean not being afraid to make your voice heard.

When each of these women saw a barrier, they didn't back down because they knew that the only way to make change is to be brave and not accept things as they are just because it's how it's always been. Most importantly, they knew that the changes they were making weren't just for their benefit, but for those that come after. And that fueled them even more.

In my observations and own experience, I looked for opportunities in which I, and these women, practiced bravery. These habits were evident, and I believe when practiced, can lead to a place in everyone's lives where brave truly becomes a verb.

1. **Embrace Fear**

   In Chapter Seven we talked about this idea of embracing fear and allowing ourselves to be OK with being fearful. Because in our fear lies the opportunities to be brave. What I've seen in other women practicing bravery is that they don't wait to first become brave. They step out even in their fear and they take risks. Knees knocking and all, they do it anyway.

   There's no spell you can cast or class you can take to wake up one day fearless. Your only choice is to **decide** to just brave it. Take action despite your fear. Be secure in who you are and put your why before your doubts. Over time, being brave will begin to come naturally.

2. **Practice Resilience**

   Be prepared to fail, maybe even often, but never, ever, ever give up. I've watched as some of the most amazing women I've ever met have been completely brought to their knees by things outside of their control; yet they've overcome obstacles even when they were told there was no hope. There's nothing more beautiful than watching a woman find her strength and not give up. Being brave means not giving up, even when you want to, even when it seems there are no other options. Accept that failures will come. Accept that life will not always be fair or go your way—even if you're doing everything right. But decide that you're going to show up anyway, no matter how hard it is. And never give up. (Yes, Amy O'Connor, I'm talking about YOU!)

3. **Live Your Purpose**

Understanding the impact that you want to make in your world, in the whole world, by discovering your why gives you the ability to use your "why power" to have a strong sense of determination. When you're living a life aligned with your purpose you will not compromise and you're able to set boundaries that allow you to live a life of fulfillment. You become focused on what you want in life and become brave enough to take action to achieve your goals as they relate to your purpose.

4. Persevere

Do not be **dis**couraged by setbacks; instead find courage. When you make a mistake or fail, use it as an opportunity for growth and learning. Be grateful for the opportunity to try again and continue working hard. Be graceful in your failures and take ownership. When I fail at something I'll often say, "I didn't fail. I just successfully figured out a way not to do something." Brave women look for the opportunities in all circumstances and use them to keep going vs. giving up.

5. Help Other Women Win

Brave women understand that when there aren't enough seats at the table, it's time to buy a bigger table. (We all know how to find our way around Wayfair.) When women come together with common goals and determination, magic happens. Supporting other women not only benefits those you support, but also helps you to grow as an individual and leader. We need to create more opportunities for the women in our lives, whether that's through leadership or personal relationships. Love the women around you. They too have experienced many of the obstacles in life that you have. Be to others what you need someone to be for you. Use your voice for others.

6. **Be YOU**

Being authentic is the key to unlocking the bravest version of yourself. Sounds strange to have to "practice" being you, right?! But unfortunately, we all struggle with truly allowing ourselves to be our true self. Stop being the person you think people want you to be and start owning the beautiful "you" that you are. Stand up for yourself and be grounded in your beliefs, despite the times when they may be unpopular. Don't be afraid to use your voice. Some people will love you, and some may not, but I would rather have relationships with those who love me for who I am than to be afraid that people love me for who I'm not. When others don't agree with you or criticize you, stand firm in who you are. You were fearfully and wonderfully made.

7. **Take Risks**

The bravest women I know aren't afraid to take big risks. They aren't afraid to step outside their comfort zones and try things a new way, even if it means being uncomfortable. They understand that with big risk can come big reward. And if they fail, they try again. They don't fear failure; instead they view it as opportunity. They are change leaders. They understand that if something no longer serves them, then it's time to move on to something new. They don't let fear hold them captive to a life where they're not fulfilled.

8. Be An Example

Being brave means sometimes taking a path not yet traveled in order to lead by example. Brave women project confidence even in fear; they trust themselves to know that in order for anything to have ever been done, someone, at some point, had to do it first. They inspire others to do the same. They create a positive example that impacts those who come after them.

9. Be Kind

Living a brave life means not only having compassion and grace for yourself but also for others. Brave women love and accept all. They don't just stand up for themselves; they also stand up for those who can't do it for themselves. They seek to lift others up and make others feel accepted and loved regardless of background or lifestyle. They stand up for what's right, even when it doesn't benefit them. They don't judge. They're kind to themselves. They correct the negative self-talk and choose to love and accept themselves the way they love and accept others.

10. Love Yourself

You can't show up as your best self if you're not first taking care of yourself. You can't be brave if you aren't in the right mindset. You must first take care of your body and mind. Fuel yourself so that you have the ability to show up and just brave it when required. If you're tired or not feeling great, it's impossible to show up for yourself, much less others. Feed yourself words and thoughts of love and encouragement and practice a lifestyle that tells yourself "I love you."

Reflect before you Neglect.

Write here:

Based on the list above, how can you begin practicing bravery in your life?

....

....

....

....

....

....

....

Fill in the blanks:

(Who) + (Why) + (How) = Fulfillment

Me:

Amy + Worthy + Brave = Fulfillment

You:

(_____) + (_____) + (Brave) = Fulfillment

DON'T
TALK
ABOUT
IT

BE
ABOUT
IT

Is It Worth It? Let Me Work It.

At the end of the day, everything in life is a choice. Most specifically, your choice. We can choose to do the work to understand who we are, or not. We can choose to look into our past to create a better future for ourselves and others, or not. We can choose to live a life centered in purpose and impact, or not. We can choose to be brave, or not.

If we choose "or not," nothing bad may come of it, and some good will still come our way. We can choose to live a life based in purpose, impact, and bravery, and I can guarantee that there will be times that won't be easy, sometimes really hard. Life already isn't easy without trying to live centered and uncompromising in your purpose. But living a life based in those things will bring you more fulfillment and happiness.

I didn't get to where I am today because I was born with a silver spoon or because I made all the right decisions. Clearly not. Everything about my story and my past doesn't equate to the life I'm living today. But the differentiating factor for me was that I remained brave when I had to rely on my belief in my capabilities. Creativity and resourcefulness were the gifts that God gave me. I chose to use them. I chose to not let my past predict my future. I chose to decide that I was worthy. I chose to never give up on myself. I chose in the moments of my greatest fear that I was going to just brave it.

Being brave got me to where I am today but isn't what brings me fulfillment. Knowing who I am, like a real sense of who I am, and living a life that is centered in purpose around my impact why is where I not only continue to level up but also feel most fulfilled and happy. Investing in myself and my own personal growth and investing in the lives of women to help them see their true potential and value is where I find fulfillment, even when I'm tired and have too much on my plate. Understanding my impact why is what keeps me showing up to set an example in my personal relationships and set a path for others in my professional life. All aspects of my life are impacted for the better because in understanding and living my purpose I have a clear direction of what I need and want to do. And in the moments when I'm most afraid, I know I can just brave it.

Hopefully you know these things now too. If you've made it this far with me, you must be a purpose-seeker. Hopefully you've laughed a little, maybe even cried a little, felt uncomfortable at times but also inspired. But most importantly, you've discovered more about yourself than when you picked up this book.

Life is hard. From personal struggles to external pressures, the hardness of life can sometimes feel like the weight of the world on our shoulders. It's a series of tough days, moments of doubt, and obstacles that seem impossible to overcome at times. But in acknowledging the difficulty and embracing the fear it brings, there's an understanding that this is a part of human experience. But it's in the place where bravery is born and we face our challenges that we uncover our strengths and capacity for growth.

Just braving it isn't always easy but it opens doors to personal growth, opportunity, and resilience. It allows you to confront your fears, navigate challenges and embrace new opportunities. Through bravery, you gain a deeper understanding about yourself, discovering strengths and capabilities you might not have known existed. It builds confidence, fosters adaptability, and cultivates a mindset that thrives in adversity. Ultimately, the rewards of bravery extend beyond immediate circumstances, shaping a more resilient and self-assured version of yourself.

You are capable and undeniably worthy of living a life filled with fulfillment. Within you is untapped potential, waiting to be unleashed. Embrace your talents, strengths, experiences, and quirks as valuable assets that contribute to keeping you in your purpose. Recognize that your aspirations are valid, and your dreams and goals carry significance. By believing in your capabilities and acknowledging your worthiness, you lay the foundation for a life rooted in purpose and contentment. It's not about perfection but the authenticity of your efforts, staying true to who you are and having the resilience to navigate challenges. You have within you the power to shape a fulfilling life. You need to...

Just Brave It.

CHAPTER TWELVE:

A Letter To Me, An Ode To You

To the extraordinary woman reading this,

In a world that often seems heavy with expectations, I want to take a moment to remind you of the extraordinary strength that is within you. As women, we carry the weight of many roles, juggling the demands of being a mother, a friend, a daughter, a wife, an employee, a leader—sometimes all at once. The challenges we face are immense, but so is our capacity for resilience and bravery.

Embrace the stories that make you...you. The wins, the failures, and everything in between. They have laid the "foundation" for who you are today. Don't be afraid to share who you are with the world. In sharing, you help other women know they're not alone.

We've all been through some ish. But we came out on the other side. Stronger, wiser, and filled with purpose. Reflect on your stories and draw strength from all that you've overcome. You did that, no one else. YOU.

I encourage you to be a light, a leader who paves the way for the generations of women who will follow. Embrace the complexity of your identity and live in your purpose, understanding your "impact why." Your story, with all its twists and turns, is uniquely yours; don't shy away from it. Own every chapter—the triumphs and the trials—because they have shaped the incredible person you are today.

In the pursuit of a fulfilling life, be relentless. Be relentless in your pursuit of dreams, in your commitment to personal growth, and in your dedication to making a positive impact. Lift other women up; together we are stronger. Look for opportunities to extend a helping hand and share the wisdom you've gained on your journey.

Imposter syndrome and negative self-talk may try to dim your light, but remember that you are more than enough. Love yourself fiercely, flaws and all. You're deserving of every ounce of love and respect you give to others. Never forget that.

We've all experienced disappointment. Sometimes, it's disappointment in yourself, that feeling of falling short and not living up to your own expectations. Other times, it's the worry of disappointing those around you—family, friends, colleagues. Here's the thing; it happens to all of us. Life is unpredictable and sometimes we miss the mark. But here's the secret sauce; it's OK. Those moments of disappointment don't define you. Instead, they're moments for growth. Learn from them, dust yourself off, and move on. The people who truly matter will understand, forgive, and support you. Give yourself grace, in the same way that you give grace to others and know that resilience comes from the moments where we overcome the disappointments in our lives.

Remember that you're never less than anyone else. The world may try to impose limits and boundaries, but know this: You are not only capable but inherently worthy. Your worth isn't defined by the expectations placed upon you. You bring unique gifts and perspectives to the table and your voice deserves to be heard. Stand tall, knowing that your worth is immeasurable, and your potential is limitless.

In moments of doubt, when the challenges seem insurmountable, remember this: "Just brave it."

Bravery isn't the absence of fear; it's the courage to face it head-on. You're capable of overcoming anything that stands in your way. Don't give up on your dreams, your aspirations, or yourself. Ever. When life gets crazy, breathe, embrace fear, and trust yourself.

So, dear friend, embrace your stories, stand firm in who you are, own your purpose, be brave, love one another, and, most importantly, love yourself. You are an inspiration for those who come behind you. Together, we can create a world where every woman is empowered to live authentically, love deeply, and "just brave it."

I love you beyond measure.

Amy Druhot

Jeremiah 29:11

Chapter One:

- Friedrich Nietzsche quote, "He who has a *why* to live for can bear almost any *how*."

Chapter Two:

- "That must make us..." skit, by Amy Druhot, Summer Jowett and Rebecca Davis

Chapter Four:

- Missy Elliot Technique inspired by THE Missy "Misdemeanor" Elliot song "Work It" by Melissa Elliot and Timothy "Timberland" Mosley, 2002.

Chapter Six:

- Worthy definition from Oxford Languages (languages.oup.com)
- SheSpeaks Study (www.shespeaks.com)

Chapter Seven:

- Decision Making Studies article "How to Make Great Decisions (Most of the Time)" by Kevin Daum (www.inc.com)
- Imposter Syndrome Studies (www.ksat.com)

- Neurobiology Fear studies- Dr. Kerry J. Ressler, MD, PhD, CSO (www.Mcleanhospital.com)
- Neil Gaiman, author of "Coraline," quote "Being brave doesn't mean you aren't scared. Being brave means you are scared, really scared, badly scared, and you do the right thing anyway."
- Gender Decision Article by Ilan Shrira (www.scientificamerican.com)
- University of Warwick Study on Gender Roles in Decision Making (www.warwick.ac.uk)
- Brave Studies in Men and Women (www.professionalsecurity.co.uk)

Chapter Ten:
- "US News" 2021 Women in executive roles studies (www.usnews.com)
- Harvard Law Review Research(www.harvardlaw.com)

The Rest:
- Just little ole me (www.amydruhot.com)

About the Author

Amy Druhot is a self-proclaimed brave expert, a title she earned through years of mastering the art of courage while secretly battling the occasional spider in her home. Born in the heart of Alabama, she bravely ventured to Virginia in her teens, a move she now credits as the catalyst for her fearless attitude—because let's face it, transitioning from sweet tea to iced tea is no small feat.

As the Vice President of Sales in the new construction industry, she's no stranger to navigating through blueprints, but her real expertise lies in the art of braving it through life. Amy fearlessly navigates boardrooms and construction sites alike, breaking gender barriers and advocating for women in a traditionally male-dominated field.

She graduated from... Oh wait, that's right, she didn't... Now, you might be wondering how someone with no college degree and questionable high school graduation credentials ended up at the top of the corporate ladder. Well, dear reader, you'll just have to dive into the pages of the book to unravel that mystery.

Thirteen years ago, Amy was scrubbing floors and cleaning houses. Today, she proudly sits as a Vice President for a top 5 builder in her market. How did she get there? Simple—she just braved it.

Recognized as Woman of the Year in Virginia for her industry, Amy's dream is to inspire women to see their full potential, embrace their worthiness, and boldly choose a life filled with fulfillment, all while bravely facing the challenges that stand in their way.

With her unique blend of humor, wisdom, and a dash of southern charm, her book promises to be a tell all journey through her life, proving that sometimes all it takes is a little bravery to build your way to the top.

Milton Keynes UK
Ingram Content Group UK Ltd.
UKHW020411080524
442319UK00005B/60